TECHNICAL REPORT

The Use of Standardized Scores in Officer Career Management and Selection

Anny Wong, Kirsten M. Keller, Carra S. Sims,
Brian McInnis, Abigail Haddad, Kate Giglio,
Nelson Lim

Prepared for the Office of the Secretary of Defense

Approved for public release; distribution unlimited

 NATIONAL DEFENSE RESEARCH INSTITUTE

The research described in this report was prepared for the Office of the Secretary of Defense (OSD). The research was conducted within the RAND National Defense Research Institute, a federally funded research and development center sponsored by OSD, the Joint Staff, the Unified Combatant Commands, the Navy, the Marine Corps, the defense agencies, and the defense Intelligence Community under Contract W74V8H-06-C-0002.

Library of Congress Cataloging-in-Publication Data is available for this publication.

ISBN: 978-0-8330-5902-4

The RAND Corporation is a nonprofit institution that helps improve policy and decisionmaking through research and analysis. RAND's publications do not necessarily reflect the opinions of its research clients and sponsors.

RAND® is a registered trademark.

Published 2012 by the RAND Corporation
1776 Main Street, P.O. Box 2138, Santa Monica, CA 90407-2138
1200 South Hayes Street, Arlington, VA 22202-5050
4570 Fifth Avenue, Suite 600, Pittsburgh, PA 15213-2665
RAND URL: http://www.rand.org/
To order RAND documents or to obtain additional information, contact
Distribution Services: Telephone: (310) 451-7002;
Fax: (310) 451-6915; Email: order@rand.org

Preface

The purpose of the project "The Use of Standardized Scores in Officer Career Management and Selection" was to examine how the use of standardized test scores in selection decisions can affect the representation of racial/ethnic minorities in key officer career fields. Because we were not able to obtain data essential to directly examine this issue, this technical report presents key considerations regarding the use of standardized tests in selection decisions, including predictive validity, bias, and adverse impact. It also documents how standardized tests are currently being used by the Department of Defense in selecting applicants into officer commissioning programs, into key career fields, and for promotion, based on information we were able to collect in fiscal year (FY) 2009–2010. In Appendix A, we also provide an overview of recent research examining the predictive validity and mean score racial/ethnic group differences on each of the standardized tests we identified. In Appendix B, we present questions for consideration by the services. Together, the report with its appendixes provides a foundation for future work examining the use of standardized tests in officer selection decisions and the impact that their use could have on the representation of racial/ethnic minorities in key officer career fields. Related RAND research has yielded the following publications:

- Beth J. Asch, Christopher Buck, Jacob Alex Klerman, Meredith Kleykamp, and David S. Loughran, *Military Enlistment of Hispanic Youth: Obstacles and Opportunities*, Santa Monica, Calif.: RAND Corporation, MG-773-OSD, 2009
- Beth J. Asch, Paul Heaton, and Bogdan Savych, *Recruiting Minorities: What Explains Recent Trends in the Army and Navy?* Santa Monica, Calif.: RAND Corporation, MG-861-OSD, 2009
- Chaitra M. Hardison, Carra S. Sims, and Eunice C. Wong, *The Air Force Officer Qualifying Test: Validity, Fairness, and Bias*, Santa Monica, Calif.: RAND Corporation, TR-744-AF, 2010
- M. Rebecca Kilburn, Lawrence M. Hanser, and Jacob Alex Klerman, *Estimating AFQT Scores for National Educational Longitudinal Study (NELS) Respondents*, Santa Monica, Calif.: RAND Corporation, MR-818-OSD/A, 1998
- Nelson Lim, Jefferson P. Marquis, Kimberly Curry Hall, David Schulker, and Xiaohui Zhuo, *Officer Classification and the Future of Diversity Among Senior Military Leaders: A Case Study of the Army ROTC*, Santa Monica, Calif.: RAND Corporation, TR-731-OSD, 2009
- Bruce R. Orvis, Michael Childress, and J. Michael Polich, *Effect of Personnel Quality on the Performance of Patriot Air Defense System Operators*, Santa Monica, Calif.: RAND Corporation, R-3901-A, 1992

- John D. Winkler, Judith C. Fernandez, and J. Michael Polich, *Effect of Aptitude on the Performance of Army Communications Operators*, Santa Monica, Calif.: RAND Corporation, R-4143-A, 1992.

This research was sponsored by the Office of the Secretary of Defense, Office of Diversity Management and Equal Opportunity (ODMEO), and conducted within the Forces and Resources Policy Center of the RAND National Defense Research Institute, a federally funded research and development center sponsored by the Office of the Secretary of Defense, the Joint Staff, the Unified Combatant Commands, the Navy, the Marine Corps, the defense agencies, and the defense Intelligence Community.

For more information on the RAND Forces and Resources Policy Center, see http://www.rand.org/nsrd/ndri/centers/frp.html or contact the director (contact information is provided on the web page).

Contents

Figure and Tables

Figure

Tables

Summary

The U.S. armed forces have long recognized the importance of selecting and promoting the most qualified individuals to serve as officers. Standardized test scores have helped military leaders assess, with a fair degree of reliability, the leadership potential and future performance of a large number of individuals at once. Currently, our research finds that the U.S. armed forces use a combination of 19 standardized tests for the purpose of selection into officer commissioning programs, for assignment to career fields, and for commissioning.[1] The tests generally fall into two broad categories: those that gauge level of knowledge or aptitude and those that gauge level of physical fitness. As for promotion, we do not find evidence indicating required use of standardized test scores.

This report provides an overview of how these tests are used as part of a broader selection system for each of the services at different points in an officer's career. The report also provides a discussion of key issues that should be considered when using standardized tests, including the relationship between a particular type of standardized test, aptitude tests, and racial/ethnic group differences, which could affect minority representation within the officer corps.

This study began with a review of the available literature on what and how standardized tests are used in the military, including peer-review published articles and reports on military testing and relevant literature in industrial and organizational psychology and educational testing. We also used Department of Defense and service policy documents, both online and printed, to identify standardized tests currently in use to select applicants for officer commissioning programs; branch, specialty, or job assignment; commissioning; and promotion. Finally, we obtained information and verified data through discussions with service representatives responsible for developing these tests or using them to inform selection decisions.

The Military Uses Standardized Testing as Part of Assessing the Whole Person at Various Points Along an Officer's Career Path

Overall, we found that standardized test scores are only one part of the military's holistic or "whole person" approach to assessing individuals for entrance into officer commissioning programs and key career fields. Interviews, performance evaluations, academic grade point average (GPA), and recommendations are also factored into final selections and appointments. The

---

[1] Note that, in this report, the terms *test*, *standardized test*, *measure*, and *assessment* are used interchangeably. Although they are separate tests, we count all standardized tests given in the Marine Corps's Basic School (TBS) as a single test in the number reported here.

types of standardized tests used also vary according to each decision point and by each service. Without data, we were unable to empirically examine the extent to which standardized tests affect selection decisions. However, according to the information available to us, standardized tests appear to play a large role in selection into officer commissioning programs and for selection into aviation careers in each of the services but not for other careers, commissioning, or promotion. What tests are utilized at different major selection points is reviewed in full in Chapter Three of the report. Appendix A provides a brief overview of each test and documents research examining the predictive validity and mean racial/ethnic group differences in scores for each of the tests we identified.

Although the RAND team was able to determine what standardized tests were called for by each service at each career decision point, due to our inability to fill some information gaps for some of the commissioning sources, some uncertainties remain as to how standardized test scores are used in various selection decisions and how they function as part of the larger selection system. In particular, we could not find direct answers to the following critical questions for certain selection processes:

- What other factors, in addition to standardized test scores, are considered as part of the selection decision for officer commissioning programs and branch, specialty, or job assignment?
- What weight do standardized test scores and other factors carry in the selection decision for officer commissioning programs and branch, specialty, or job assignment?
- How often are tests waived, for whom, and under what circumstances? Is there a replacement for these tests?

The difficulty in finding answers to these questions is likely due to a lack of publicly available information or published material on these selection processes and requirements. To help fill in these remaining information gaps for research and public information and to promote greater transparency regarding selection decisions, we suggest that the Office of the Secretary of Defense (OSD) ask the services to provide detailed specifics on their selection systems. Toward that end, this report includes a list of questions for the services and officer commissioning sources (Appendix B).

Acknowledgments

We thank Clarence A. Johnson, principal director of ODMEO, OSD, for his support and assistance in this research. We also thank James Love of ODMEO and many other individuals who helped us gain access to research data and provided us valuable input: RAND Air Force Fellows Lt Col Jeffrey S. Brown, Maj Tracy Bunko, Lt Col Robert Fabian, Col Scott Guermonprez, Col Jeanne Hardrath, Col Thomas P. Hesterman, Maj Ken Kuebler, and Trish Ross; at the Air Force Research Laboratory, Thomas R. Carretta; at Headquarters Air Force Recruiting Service, Paul Ditullio, chief of market research and analysis; at Air Force Personnel Center, Kenneth Schwartz, chief of strategic research and assessment, and Johnny Weissmuller; at Air Force Manpower and Personnel (AF/A1), Force Management Policy, Lisa Hughes; RAND Army Fellows LTC Kevin Kawasaki and LTC José Madera; at U.S. Army Cadet Command, LTC Rodney Roederer, chief of the Operations Analysis Division, and Craig Zeitler, Accessions and Security Division; with the U.S. Marine Corps, LtCol Julia Meade and Col Otto J. Rutt; at Marine Corps Recruiting Command, LtCol Chester McMillon, head of officer programs; at the U.S. Naval Academy, CDR Craig Doxey, chair of professional programs, and Glen Gottschalk, director of institutional research; and, at the Naval Aerospace Medical Institute, LCDR Henry Phillips, head of the Department of Operational Psychology.

We also thank our RAND colleagues Bruce Orvis and Chaitra Hardison for their insightful comments and helpful suggestions in reviewing this document. We regret any omission and sincerely thank all who have helped us.

Abbreviations

AFAST	Alternate Flight Aptitude Selection Test
AFOQT	Air Force Officer Qualifying Test
AFQT	Armed Forces Qualification Test
AFROTC	U.S. Air Force Reserve Officer Training Corps
AFRS	Air Force Recruiting Service
ALCPT	American Language Course Placement Test
APFT	Army Physical Fitness Test
API	Aviation Pre-Flight Indoctrination
AQR	Academic Qualifications Rating
ASTB	Aviation Selection Test Battery
ASVAB	Armed Services Vocational Aptitude Battery
CFA	Candidate Fitness Assessment
CFT	Combat Fitness Test
CLEP	College-Level Examination Program
CPR	Cadet Performance Rank
DoD	U.S. Department of Defense
ECLT	English Comprehension Level Test
EOD	explosive ordnance disposal
FOFAR	Flight Officer Flight Aptitude Rating
FY	fiscal year
GED	General Educational Development Test
GMAT	Graduate Management Admission Test
GPA	grade point average

GRE	Graduate Record Examination
GT	General Technical
IQ	intelligence quotient
LSAT	Law School Admission Test
MCO	Marine Corps order
MEPS	Military Entrance Processing Station
MOS	military occupational specialty
NFO	Naval Flight Officer
NROTC	Naval Reserve Officers Training Corps
OAR	Officer Aptitude Rating
OCC	Officer Candidate Course
OCS	Officer Candidate School
ODMEO	Office of Diversity Management and Equal Opportunity
OML	order of merit list
OMS	order of merit score
OPNAV	Chief of Naval Operations
OSD	Office of the Secretary of Defense
OTS	Officer Training School
PCSM	Pilot Candidate Selection Method
PFAR	Pilot Flight Aptitude Rating
PFE	physical fitness exam
PFT	physical fitness test
PLC	Platoon Leaders Class
PNS	professor of naval science
PRT	physical readiness test
RL	restricted line
ROTC	Reserve Officer Training Corps
TAPAS	Tailored Adaptive Personality Assessment System
TBAS	Test of Basic Aviation Skills
TBS	(the) Basic School

URL	unrestricted line
USAFA	U.S. Air Force Academy
USCGA	U.S. Coast Guard Academy
USMA	U.S. Military Academy
USNA	U.S. Naval Academy

CHAPTER ONE

Introduction

The U.S. Department of Defense (DoD), like other employers, uses a range of tools to select qualified applicants for admission to officer commissioning programs, specialized training, and career advancement opportunities in the U.S. armed forces. Among these tools are standardized tests, which have a long history of use in the U.S. military. In fact, the Army, in its effort to rapidly screen individuals for eligibility to serve in the military, made the first wide-scale use of standardized tests (in this case, intelligence quotient, or IQ, tests) in World War I. In the decades that followed, the U.S. armed forces rapidly expanded the variety and use of standardized tests not only to screen for eligible recruits but also to determine mastery of knowledge and skills by military personnel and potential for success in training programs.[1]

This use of standardized tests has raised some concerns and criticism, however, particularly regarding the use of standardized aptitude tests, considering that research shows that aptitude test scores tend to show significant racial/ethnic group differences. Specifically, studies show that, on average, blacks and Hispanics tend to score lower than their white counterparts.[2] Thus, critics assert that a heavy reliance on standardized aptitude tests in selection decisions could negatively affect the racial/ethnic diversity of officers, as well as minority representation in certain career fields. Nevertheless, research also finds that well-developed standardized aptitude tests are the best single predictor of future performance, resulting in what is known as a *diversity-validity dilemma.*[3]

The original goal of this study was, therefore, to examine how the use of standardized test scores (aptitude tests and other types of standardized tests) in selection decisions can affect the representation of racial/ethnic minorities in key officer career fields. However, we were not able to obtain essential data from the services to directly examine this issue. Therefore, this report utilizes information we were able to collect to build a foundation for future studies by documenting how standardized test scores are used by the services in selecting applicants for entrance into officer commissioning programs; branch, specialty, or occupation assignments; commissioning; and promotion opportunities. We also discuss key considerations regarding the use of standardized tests in selection decisions, including predictive validity, bias, and adverse impact. In Appendix A, we provide an overview of recent research examining the predictive validity and mean score racial/ethnic group differences on each of the standardized tests we identified as being in current use by the services.

---

[1] Edwards, 2006.

[2] Sackett, Borneman, and Connelly, 2008.

[3] Pyburn, Ployhart, and Kravitz, 2008.

Study Scope and Research Method

This report covers all five services: Army, Navy, Air Force, Marine Corps, and Coast Guard. We focused on standardized tests that are explicitly called for by DoD or the services for use in selection of applicants into officer commissioning programs; branch, specialty, or job assignments; commissioning; and promotion opportunities. Officer commissioning programs include the Reserve Officer Training Corps (ROTC) programs, officer candidate schools (OCSs) or Officer Training School (OTS), and the service academies.[4] Although ROTC is the largest source of commissioning officers, the importance of other commissioning sources is not insignificant. Also, the Marine Corps does not have its own ROTC program or service academy and instead utilizes the Navy's programs. As a result, the majority of officer accessions for the Marine Corps come from its OCS programs.[5] Similarly, the Coast Guard does not have a ROTC program, relying instead on the U.S. Coast Guard Academy (USCGA) and its OCS for officer production.

This research began with a review of the available literature on what and how standardized tests are being used in the military. Our literature review included peer-reviewed published articles and reports on military testing and relevant literature in industrial and organizational psychology and educational testing. We also utilized DoD and service policy documents and online and printed resources from each of the services to identify the standardized tests currently used to select applicants for officer commissioning programs; branch, specialty, or job assignments; commissioning; and promotion opportunities. Finally, we obtained information and verified the data through discussions with service representatives responsible for developing the standardized tests or using them to inform selection decisions.

Organization of This Report

This report contains four chapters. Chapter Two provides an overview of standardized tests and considerations for their use in personnel selection in general. Chapter Three presents our findings on what standardized tests are currently used by the services and how the test scores are used in selection decisions. Finally, Chapter Four presents our conclusions. This report also contains two appendixes. Appendix A provides an overview of each standardized test currently being used by the services and discusses research on the predictive validity and racial/ethnic group differences for each test. Appendix B then provides a list of questions relevant to each of the services regarding key information gaps that remain in understanding their selection systems and the role of standardized tests.

---

[4] As is explained in detail in Chapter Three, this report does not cover direct commissioned officers because they are not required to enter officer commissioning programs before they are given commissions in the military. Further, the only standardized test required for direct commission applicants is a service-specific physical fitness test.

[5] Other than those who commission via the U.S. Naval Academy, all officer candidates must complete commissioning programs at the Marine Corps OCS. These courses or programs can last between six and 12 weeks. For example, non–prior enlisted persons already holding a bachelor's degree from an accredited institution can directly apply to enroll in the ten-week commissioning program. By comparison, a student in his or her junior or senior undergraduate program can enroll in the ten-week Platoon Leaders Class during the summer and return to his or her university to complete the bachelor's degree before gaining his or her commission. An undergraduate student in the Navy ROTC program who opts to join the Marine Corps must also complete a six-week program at OCS and complete his or her undergraduate program before he or she is commissioned. See Office of the Under Secretary of Defense, 2010, and U.S. Marine Corps, undated (b).

CHAPTER TWO

Use of Standardized Tests

This chapter presents a definition of *standardized test*, the criteria for what makes a good standardized test, and relevant issues regarding racial/ethnic group differences, bias, and adverse impact. We provide the information in this chapter given its relevance to understanding standardized tests in general, as well as due to the study's original intent of focusing on minority representation. Published research related to these issues is then presented in Appendix A for each of the standardized tests we identified.

What Is a Standardized Test?

Commonly, the term *standardized test* is used to refer to tests measuring ability, aptitude, or achievement, such as the SAT exam.[1] However, the definition of *standardized test* is actually much broader and encompasses any test in which individuals' responses are scored and evaluated in a consistent manner.[2] Therefore, testing experts also use the term *standardized test* to refer to measures of "attitudes, interests, personality, cognitive functioning, and mental health" that are scored and evaluated in a consistent manner.[3] Throughout this report, we use this broader definition to examine the standardized tests currently being used by the services. However, we find that the majority of the standardized tests identified measure level of aptitude.

What Makes a Good Standardized Test?

For test scores to be useful in selecting the best possible candidates, a test must be both reliable and valid. *Reliability* refers to the extent to which a test is consistent, and *validity* refers to the extent to which a test is accurate at measuring the underlying construct, as well as the accurateness of inferences made based on test data.

---

[1] SAT is a registered trademark of the College Board.

[2] American Educational Research Association, American Psychological Association, and National Council on Measurement in Education Joint Committee on Standards for Educational and Psychological Testing, 1999.

[3] American Educational Research Association, American Psychological Association, and National Council on Measurement in Education Joint Committee on Standards for Educational and Psychological Testing, 1999.

Reliability

When we say that a test is reliable, we mean that the test is free from random error and will produce similar results in repeated administrations. There are multiple ways to examine reliability. One common way is to examine the consistency of individuals' test scores over time. A reliable test is consistent and, through repetitions, maintains a level of score stability. Although test items (questions) and distracters (e.g., incorrect answers on a multiple-choice test) can change, a reliable test will evaluate the same set of abilities in the same way and produce a similar score over successive test administrations.[4]

Validity

Validity is the sine qua non of employment testing. Although the objective of this research was not to examine test validity specifically, validity is pertinent to this research and deserves our attention. In the selection context, researchers most often examine what is known as *predictive* or *criterion-related* validity.[5] It is the extent to which a predictor, such as test performance, is related to a criterion of interest. For example, given that the SAT exam is often used to select students for admission to college, one might be interested in knowing whether the SAT exam actually predicts how well students perform academically in college (e.g., academic grade point average [GPA]). Predictive validity in this case can be ascertained by examining the extent to which SAT exam scores are related to actual student GPA in college.

The most common way to assess predictive validity is to examine the correlation or degree of association between scores on the test and the criterion of interest (e.g., performance, turnover).[6] Correlations range from −1 to 1, with a correlation at either end of this range indicating that the test in question perfectly predicts the criterion of interest. A correlation of 0 means that there is no relationship between the test score and the criterion of interest. In the selection context, correlations are generally expressed in positive terms (and therefore range from 0 to 1), such that, as a test score goes up, the criterion of interest, such as job performance, increases. In other words, better test scores are related to better job performance. The more strongly correlated (that is, the closer to 1) a test is with the criterion of interest, the more useful it is at predicting the criterion of interest, and the fewer mistakes it makes in prediction.

However, in practice, no test can predict perfectly. Many factors can influence the particular criterion of interest. As an example, job performance can be influenced by factors, such as workspace and equipment, management style, and workplace atmosphere, that are often beyond the control of the individual. As noted by Schmidt and Hunter in their analysis of the many decades of research on selection tools, a test with a correlation of about 0.5 is at the high end of potential validity.[7] Further, even tests whose validity is lower (at or above 0.3) can be quite helpful and considerably lower the number of mistakes made in selection.

---

[4]   It is possible that learning can occur between the initial test period and the retest, resulting in a change in the "true score." Therefore, this definition of reliability assumes that test scores will be similar as long as there has been no change in the "true score" or "performance level."

[5]   N. Schmitt and Chan, 1998.

[6]   N. Schmitt and Chan, 1998.

[7]   Schmidt and Hunter, 1998.

Racial/Ethnic Group Differences, Bias, and Adverse Impact

Although reliability and validity are two basic criteria in assessing the quality of standardized tests, experts have also called attention to the importance of being aware of potential racial/ethnic group differences, bias, and adverse impact in the use of standardized tests.[8]

Racial/Ethnic Differences

Some well-known standardized tests, particularly aptitude tests, consistently show mean score racial/ethnic group differences. On average, Hispanics and blacks tend to have lower mean scores than whites have.[9] Although an examination of gender difference is beyond the scope of the current study, it is important to note that there are also some differences by gender, with women often scoring slightly higher than men on verbal ability, and men scoring slightly higher than women on quantitative ability. However, variability has been observed in these gender differences across studies and subtests.[10] Overall, the existence of these mean differences often leads to the question of whether standardized aptitude tests are biased or discriminate against racial/ethnic minorities.

Bias

Evidence of demographic differences alone does not mean that a test is biased. In a selection and staffing context, testing standards (e.g., see *Standards for Educational and Psychological Testing*) indicate that bias is most commonly examined by considering the relationship between a test score and a criterion, such as job performance.[11] Bias is present when test scores predict the criterion of interest (e.g., future performance) differently for one group than for another group.[12] A test is considered to be biased against a group if it *underpredicts* how members of the group will perform in the future. In other cases, a test can actually favor members of a group and *overpredict* how members of that group will perform in the future. In general, research has found that well-developed standardized aptitude tests are not biased against racial/ethnic minorities.[13]

Adverse Impact

The Uniform Guidelines on Employee Selection Procedures were promulgated to provide employers with guidance on how to apply Title VII of the Civil Rights Act in their organizations.[14] Adverse or disparate impact is one type of discrimination that is addressed under Title VII, the federal law that prohibits most workplace harassment and discrimination in all

---

[8] For a more thorough treatment of these issues, with specific illustrations using the context of selection in the Air Force, see Hardison, Sims, and Wong, 2010.

[9] Sackett, Schmitt, et al., 2001.

[10] Sackett, Borneman, and Connelly, 2008.

[11] American Educational Research Association, American Psychological Association, and National Council on Measurement in Education Joint Committee on Standards for Educational and Psychological Testing, 1999.

[12] Cleary, 1968.

[13] Sackett, Schmitt, et al., 2001.

[14] 29 U.S.C. 1607.1–1607.18. Although Title VII may not apply to members of the U.S. armed forces, the services typically adhere to its guidance. Also, the armed services are required under the Fourteenth Amendment to give equal protection to all groups and individuals regardless of race (*U.S. v. Virginia*, 518 U.S. 515, 1996).

private employers, state and local governments, and educational institutions with 15 or more employees.

Adverse impact is said to occur when an employment practice that appears neutral (i.e., shows no intent to discriminate) results in the proportion of applicants that is hired or accepted from a protected group being less than four-fifths (80 percent) of the proportion of applicants that is hired or accepted from the group with the highest selection rate (usually, white or male applicants). This is commonly termed the *four-fifths rule*.[15] However, the existence of adverse or disparate impact does not mean that an organization is applying unlawfully discriminatory practices. Adverse impact is not considered unlawful discrimination if the selection measure can be demonstrated to be a valid predictor of an important job-related outcome, such as performance. Thus, a test that results in adverse impact is still considered legal if it is supported by evidence that it is a significant predictor of important job-related outcomes and it can be shown that there is no equally effective but less discriminatory test available.[16] In the case of well-developed standardized aptitude tests, although they show mean score racial/ethnic group differences, research has also found that they are the single best predictor of performance across a variety of different jobs.[17] Therefore, the use of standardized aptitude tests does not generally violate Title VII.

Organizations have the right (and, one would argue, the responsibility, in the case of taxpayer-funded organizations, such as the military) to select the best people for the job. When a selection test can help make that selection decision more accurately, the organization can and should use it to do so. If it is possible to ameliorate the effects of group differences without sacrificing validity and subsequently incurring the expense of costly selection errors, the organization should also do so.

Standardized Tests Are Generally Used as Part of a Selection System

The foregoing discussion on the issues of standardized testing—in particular, the sections on racial/ethnic group differences, bias, and adverse impact—principally deals with standardized tests in isolation. However, standardized tests are not generally used in isolation but are part of a broader selection system. In fact, as the next chapter shows, the services all emphasize a holistic or "whole person" approach in selection decisions, so that candidates are assessed based on several different factors, including standardized tests, along with interviews and performance evaluations. This whole-person approach also allows the services flexibility in their scoring systems by giving them the ability to adjust a total score up or down based on other qualitative information that might not be factored into the original quantitative scoring method.

If a test is used together with other tools, it should also be examined together with these tools. For example, even if certain tools have been shown to be valid on their own, if these tools are paired with other tools whose validity is unknown, the validity of the entire system is unknown. Similarly, the weight each tool is given toward the final decision can significantly influence the overall validity and resulting racial/ethnic differences of the selection system as a

---

[15] 29 U.S.C. 1607.1–1607.18.

[16] Civil Rights Act of 1991, Pub. L. 102-166, 1991.

[17] Schmidt and Hunter, 1998.

whole. Furthermore, using several different selection tools as part of a whole selection system can help ameliorate the potential adverse impact that often arises with the use of standardized aptitude tests. As discussed previously, the standardized tests used most commonly in selection decisions are aptitude tests because they have been found to be the single best predictor of future training success and job performance. They are also easy to administer and cost-effective for organizations that are dealing with a large number of applicants, such as the military.[18] However, standardized aptitude tests tend to show racial/ethnic group differences, resulting in what is known as a *diversity-validity dilemma*.[19] One suggested solution for addressing this dilemma is to supplement these tests with alternative selection tools, such as structured interviews, or noncognitive standardized tests, such as standardized personality measures, which produce less adverse impact but still have good predictive validity (although not as strong as aptitude tests).[20] Therefore, it is important to examine not only the standardized tests used by the U.S. armed forces but also how these tests are used as part of a broader selection system.

As previously indicated, we were not able to obtain data essential to assessing how the use of standardized tests by the services might be affecting the representation of racial/ethnic minorities in key career fields and the overall officer corps. Therefore, Chapter Three provides an overview of what standardized tests are currently being used by the services and how they are being used as part of a broader selection system, according to information we were able to collect. By doing so, this report builds a foundation for future research to examine representation issues. (Appendix A presents research on the predictive validity and racial/ethnic group differences for each test identified.)

---

[18] Schmidt and Hunter, 1998.

[19] Pyburn, Ployhart, and Kravitz, 2008.

[20] One example of standardized personality measures is one that the Army is currently developing, the Tailored Adaptive Personality Assessment System (TAPAS), which could be used in selection decisions and would have less adverse impact. On the adverse impact and predictive validity of alternative selection tools, see Ployhart and Holtz, 2008.

CHAPTER THREE

Current Use of Standardized Tests in the Armed Forces

This chapter presents what we found on what and how standardized tests are currently used in the services. Much of the information gathered has relied on secondary sources. Several service representatives verified the information collected and filled information gaps to complete the picture of what and how tests are used by the services.

The U.S. armed forces, with their need to assess large numbers of individuals at once, has a long history of standardized testing. Starting in World War I, there was a major attempt to incorporate mental testing into the Army selection process: About 1.8 million men took either the Alpha test, for those who were literate, or the Beta test, for those who were not literate or who were less fluent English speakers. Personality testing was also incorporated via the Woodworth Personality Data Sheet, and aptitude testing was used in officer selection. After World War I, testing was scaled down but continued for men of "uncertain literacy."[1]

During World War II, standardized testing again gained widespread use. More than 12 million soldiers and marines took the Army General Classification Test for classification and officer selection. This test assessed verbal, arithmetic, and spatial elements, and scores were numerical and categorical, similar to today's Armed Services Vocational Aptitude Battery (ASVAB). The Army Ground and Service Forces required a minimum score for admission to their OCS, as did the Army Air Forces for flight officers, pilots, navigators, and bombardiers. The Army also used a psychomotor test in pilot selection.[2] Finally, the Navy used the Navy General Classification Test, a group verbal test that aided the classification of 3 million sailors into jobs.[3]

In 1948, Congress passed the Selective Service Act, which mandated DoD to develop an aptitude screening test for use by all the services.[4] DoD responded with the Armed Forces Qualification Test (AFQT), which contained questions testing vocabulary, arithmetic, spatial relationships, and mechanical ability. Each branch of the military set its own minimum requirements. In 1976, the ASVAB, with the AFQT incorporated into it, began to be used by all of the services for selection.[5] The ASVAB has evolved over the years, adding or subtracting

---

[1] Kevles, 1968.

[2] Harrell, 1992.

[3] Lewinski and Galway, 1945; Brodnick and Ree, 1997.

[4] Pub. L. 80-759, 1948.

[5] Moore, 2009.

subtests.[6] Other standardized tests designed to measure aptitude levels and relevant skills and knowledge have also been developed by the services for use in selection.

Current Practices in Standardized Testing

The information we collected suggests that a combination of 19 standardized tests is used by the U.S. armed forces for various selection decisions throughout an officer's career.[7] The tests generally fall into two broad categories: those that gauge level of knowledge or aptitude and those that gauge physical fitness. As discussed previously, standardized tests are used as one component of larger selection systems. Other tools and measures, such as interviews, GPA, performance ratings, and recommendations, are also factored into the final selection decision. As we discuss in more detail later in this chapter, the information we gathered also indicates that, although various standardized tests are used for selection purposes, generally only a few are mandatory for all applicants. How test scores are used also varies across the services. On one end are instances in which the test score is the most critical determinant for selection. On the other end are instances in which the test score is only one of many selection criteria and substitutions or waivers are permitted.

Overall, the findings indicate that selection into officer commissioning programs is based on a holistic or "whole-person" evaluation of candidates using standardized test scores and other factors, such as GPA, college major, performance evaluations, and interview ratings. However, we were unable to find detailed official weighting systems for these selection systems. Information we gathered suggests to us that the whole-person approach to selection also seems to allow considerable flexibility for the selection board to add or subtract points, based on qualitative information that might not be factored into the original quantitative scoring method, to applicants' overall scores. From the information we gathered, we were also not able to determine the extent to which many tests are being used only to disqualify those below the official cutoff scores rather than to also judge among qualified candidates. Finally, our information indicates that some of these tests can be waived, and it is likely that waivers vary across tests, usage, and military demand at the time of selection. However, we could not find data on how widespread or under what circumstances waiving occurs for many of these tests.

In this chapter, we present an overview of the standardized tests that are required by the services, along with descriptions of how they are used in selection decisions. The chapter begins with a description of the conceptual framework we used to examine how tests are utilized by the services. It is followed by four subsections detailing the use of standardized test scores in selecting applicants for (1) officer commissioning programs; (2) branch, specialty, or jobs; (3) commissions; and (4) promotions. In the first two subsections, three pathways through which individuals can become military officers—ROTC, OCS or OTS, and the service academies—further divide our descriptions.

---

[6]   Mayberry and Hiatt, 1992.

[7]   Although they are separate tests, we count all standardized tests given in the Marine Corps's Basic School (TBS) as a single test in the number reported here.

Conceptual Framework

Our research to determine what standardized tests the services use for selection purposes soon resulted in a mass of information. As we tried to make sense of the information collected, it became obvious that delineating what standardized tests are used as part of major selection decisions to produce commissioned officers and for career advancement would make the most sense. The first step toward becoming a military officer typically involves entry into an officer commissioning program. Whether it is the ROTC, OCS, OTS, or the service academies, one learns military history, organizations, strategy, ethos, and values and receives the necessary physical and technical training for becoming a military officer.

The only exception to this is those individuals who obtain direct commissions to join certain specialized military occupations (e.g., physicians, dentists, veterinarians, nurses, chaplains, lawyers). Their selection is primarily determined by a few requirements: (1) having the requisite four-year college and postgraduate training and license to practice, (2) meeting basic legal and age requirements (e.g., U.S. citizen, no criminal record, and between 21 and 48 years of age for Army medical officers), and (3) meeting the basic health and fitness requirements for all military officers. In fact, as direct-commissioned officers, applicants are given commissions before they are sent to their service's direct-commissioning training, called Commissioned Officer Training, Officer Development School, or Direct Commission Officer School. Thus, the idea of an officer commissioning program does not apply to these applicants. More importantly for the purpose of this study, the services require applicants for direct commissions to pass only one standardized test: a service physical fitness test. Thus, this report focuses only on three officer commissioning sources—ROTC programs, OCS or OTS, and the service academies—and examines the general path applicants would travel to advance their military careers.

With selection to enter an officer commissioning program as the first step toward becoming a military officer, Figure 3.1 illustrates the career path of a commissioned officer and highlights points at which important selection decisions are made. Each of these points represents a major gateway that an applicant must pass through if he or she is to become a commissioned officer and advance in a service career path. Thus, finding out what standardized tests are used and how they are used at each of these gateways is the focus of our research.

The first gateway is for an applicant to demonstrate eligibility for selection into an officer commissioning program. Where standardized tests are concerned, the SAT exam and the ACT are the two most common types of standardized tests used. Applicants must also pass a physical fitness test for selection into one of the three officer commissioning programs. The second gateway can be especially critical for the purpose of this report because this is when individuals in officer commissioning programs are selected for their service branch, specialty, or job.[8] In short, not only is this the first major point at which individuals are given the opportunity to pursue work in a specialized area according to their interests, but it is also the point at which they must compete for the jobs or career fields that are most selective. Performance in the officer commissioning program (e.g., in leadership and other areas), personal preferences, and service requirements all play a role, as can their scores on some special standardized tests, in selection into certain branches, specialties, or jobs. The third gateway is commission-

---

[8]   For some services and commissioning programs, selection into the officer commissioning program takes place at the same time as selection into the branch, specialty, or job.

Figure 3.1
Standardized Tests and Major Selection Points

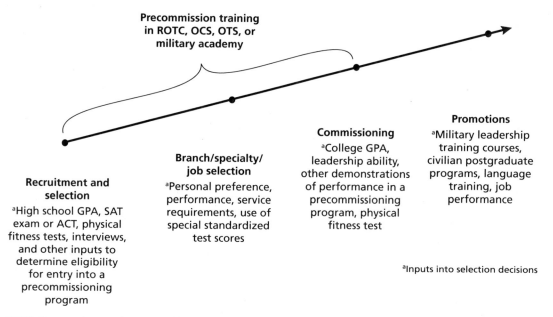

Precommission training in ROTC, OCS, OTS, or military academy

Promotions
[a]Military leadership training courses, civilian postgraduate programs, language training, job performance

Commissioning
[a]College GPA, leadership ability, other demonstrations of performance in a precommissioning program, physical fitness test

Branch/specialty/ job selection
[a]Personal preference, performance, service requirements, use of special standardized test scores

Recruitment and selection
[a]High school GPA, SAT exam or ACT, physical fitness tests, interviews, and other inputs to determine eligibility for entry into a precommissioning program

[a]Inputs into selection decisions

NOTE: Postgraduate education, skills, and experience can influence career options and advancement.
RAND TR952-3.1

ing. An individual is given a commission in the service of his or her choice in the U.S. armed forces. The individual must complete a four-year undergraduate degree and must meet all the performance requirements of the officer commissioning program. Performance is measured by various methods, including a qualitative assessment by the commanding officers of the commissioning program, GPA or performance on content-specific tests, and physical fitness test scores. Once a commissioned officer, the individual is expected to continue to grow as a leader as he or she takes on new and bigger responsibilities. Thus, promotion (the final gateway shown in Figure 3.1) requires officers to go through leadership training courses at different stages of their careers and expects postgraduate education and other skills and experiences as appropriate (e.g., field experience and proficiency in a foreign language), in addition to job performance. In the sections that follow, there are more details on the tests used at each of these major decision points.

Selection into Officer Commissioning Programs

The first step toward becoming a commissioned officer in the U.S. military is to enroll in one of three primary officer commissioning sources: ROTC, OCS or OTS, or a service academy. Each source provides a different avenue for becoming an officer, depending on one's current life and educational situation. An individual who already has a bachelor's degree must enroll in an OCS or OTS program. In contrast, an individual who has not completed a bachelor's degree can attend one of the service academies, where he or she will earn both a bachelor's degree and the commission or can attend a ROTC program while enrolled at an eligible four-year college or university. These officer commissioning programs serve to provide an introduction to military life, as well as to provide leadership and physical fitness training. After completing a bachelor's degree and the commissioning program requirements, the individual gains a commission as an officer in his or her particular service, with the rank of second lieutenant in the Army, Air Force, or Marine Corps or as an ensign in the Navy or Coast Guard.

In order to enroll in any of the officer commissioning programs, prospective applicants must meet certain minimum eligibility requirements related to age, physical fitness, moral conduct, citizenship, and academic performance. Applicants then go through a selection process in which they are competing with their peers for a limited number of slots each year. A key component of this selection process is standardized test scores, which are used along with several other factors to make final selection decisions for admission into the various programs. The following subsections provide an overview of the standardized tests used for selection into each officer commissioning program and the role these tests play in the overall selection system.

ROTC

The largest DoD-wide officer commissioning program is the ROTC program. The Army, Navy, and Air Force each has its own ROTC program, with it being the largest commissioning source for both the Army and Air Force in recent years.[9] (The Coast Guard does not run a ROTC program.) The Marine Corps does not have its own ROTC program, but it commissions officers into the Marine Corps through the Naval Reserve Officers Training Corps (NROTC) program. Enrollment in ROTC occurs while attending a four-year college or university, which is either the host of a ROTC program or has a cross-town affiliation with a host ROTC program. At a minimum, each ROTC applicant must be enrolled in an eligible college or university, be a permanent resident or citizen of the United States, be at least 17 years of age at the time of enrollment, and have a high school diploma or equivalent certificate.[10] Some students in ROTC receive merit-based scholarships toward tuition and education-related fees. These scholarships range from four-year scholarships for high school seniors to two- or three-year scholarships for students already enrolled in college. An applicant to ROTC may have no prior military experience, have prior military experience, be in the Reserves or National Guard, or be an active-duty enlisted servicemember with a recommendation from his or her commanding officer.

Where standardized tests are concerned, our research indicates that the services use the standardized tests shown in Table 3.1 to determine eligibility and final selection of applicants. In general, the standardized tests that are most common for selecting applicants are the SAT exam and ACT, which are predominantly used for scholarship selection. Admission boards consider the candidate's qualifications broadly using the whole-person concept, which includes a combination of test scores, academic background, athletic accomplishments, field of study in college, and other personal qualities. Brief descriptions for each test and how the services use them are in the sections that follow.

---

[9]   Office of the Under Secretary of Defense, 2010.

[10]   Only U.S. citizens can gain commissions as military officers and enroll in the ROTC program's advanced course, which is open to junior- and senior-year college students. Permanent residents can enroll only in the ROTC program's basic course, which is open to freshman and sophomore college students. The most common equivalency certificate is the General Educational Development Test (GED®) (U.S. Army Reserve Officer's Training Corps, undated [a]; USAFA, undated [a]; U.S. Navy, undated [a]).

Table 3.1
Tests for ROTC Applicants

Services' Tests	Army	Navy and Marine Corps	Air Force
ACT	x	x	x
AFOQT			x
Air Force PFT			x
APFT	x		
ASVAB	x	x	
Marine Corps PFT		x	
Navy PRT		x	
President's Challenge PFT	x		
SAT exam	x	x	x

NOTE: AFOQT = Air Force Officer Qualifying Test. PFT = physical fitness test.
APFT = Army Physical Fitness Test. PRT = physical readiness test.

Army. The Army ROTC program operates at more than 1,300 colleges and universities (273 host programs and more than 1,100 cross-town partnerships).[11] It has been the largest source of commissioned officers in the Army in recent years, composing roughly 35 to 40 percent of all officer accessions.[12] The Army ROTC program is broken down into two major courses: the ROTC basic course and the ROTC advanced course. The ROTC basic course is taken during the freshman and sophomore years of college and does not require a service commitment for participation. The ROTC advanced course is taken during the junior and senior years of college and requires a commitment to serve in the Army following graduation. An applicant must either have completed the ROTC basic course or have attended a four-week leadership course prior to enrolling in the advanced course. All ROTC scholarships require a service commitment.

As shown in Table 3.1, the Army uses the following standardized tests in determining eligibility for scholarship selection and enrollment into ROTC: SAT exam, ACT, ASVAB (only the General Technical [GT] score), APFT, and the President's Challenge PFT. For nonscholarship applicants, the only standardized test required is the APFT (three events: push-ups, sit-ups, and a two-mile run).[13] The applicant must receive a minimum total score of 180 (minimum of 60 in each event). This means, for example, that a male between 17 and 21 years old must be able to complete a minimum of 42 push-ups and 53 sit-ups each within one minute and complete a two-mile run in at least 15 minutes and 54 seconds; a woman needs to be able to complete 19 push-ups and 53 sit-ups each within one minute and complete a two-mile run in 18 minutes and 54 seconds. At the time of this writing, we are not aware of other factors that are used to select nonscholarship candidates for ROTC.

[11] U.S. Army, undated (b).

[12] Office of the Under Secretary of Defense, 2010.

[13] U.S. Army Recruiting Command, undated.

For scholarship applicants, a whole-person score is used as part of the selection process. Selection for four-year scholarships for graduating high school students is based on SAT exam or ACT scores (25 percent), performance in student athlete leader activities (extracurricular activities) (20 percent), professor of military science ratings (20 percent), and selection board scores (35 percent). Four-year scholarship applicants must also pass the President's Challenge PFT (three events: push-ups, sit-ups, and a one-mile run). We were not able to find the minimum passing scores required on these events, however. The applicant must also receive a minimum total score of 180 on the APFT (minimum of 60 in each event) after he or she is enrolled in college to officially enroll in the ROTC program and contract with the Army to receive the ROTC scholarship. For two- and three-year scholarship applicants, the whole-person score is based on cumulative college GPA (30 percent), student athlete leader activities (15 percent), an interview (15 percent), and selection board scores (40 percent). The applicant must also receive a minimum total score of 180 on the APFT (minimum of 60 in each event).

Finally, the Army also has a separate scholarship program, the Green to Gold program, for the active-duty enlisted soldier who wishes to earn his or her commission as an officer.[14] An enlisted soldier applicant in the Green to Gold program can apply for a four-year, three-year, or two-year ROTC scholarship. Applicants are selected based on a whole-person score composed of SAT exam or ACT scores (only for four-year scholarship applicants), the GT score from the ASVAB (a composite of the verbal expression and arithmetic reasoning scores; minimum score is 110), cumulative GPA (2.5 minimum), APFT scores (minimum of 60 in each event), and selection board scores. At the time of this writing, we are not aware of the weight given to each of these factors in the scholarship selection process, however.

As part of the Green to Gold program, there are also Hip Pocket scholarships given out to selected eligible active-duty enlisted soldiers nominated by their division commanders. The eligibility checklist for this program includes much higher requirements. The list includes having a 3.0 GPA and an SAT exam score of 1,100 (combined SAT exam math and verbal) or ACT score of 21 (composite), or minimum score of 90 in each event on the AFPT; having been awarded certain leadership positions; and having a minimum GT score of 110 on the ASVAB. However, it appears that some of these might not be strict requirements but rather are standards to which commanders should compare candidates in determining competitiveness.[15] We are also not aware of the weight given to each of these factors in the scholship selection process.

Navy. The NROTC program serves the recruitment needs of both the Navy and the Marine Corps. Currently, more than 150 colleges and universities have NROTC programs or cross-town affiliations.[16] As shown in Table 3.1, the Navy uses the following standardized tests in determining eligibility for scholarship selection and enrollment into NROTC: SAT exam or ACT, Navy PRT, and ASVAB (GT score).[17] Four-year scholarship applicants must receive minimum scores on either the SAT exam (530 English and 520 math) or ACT (22 English and 21 math) to be eligible. These minimums can be waived for a student who is within the 90th percentile of his or her graduating high school class. Applicants must also pass the Navy PRT (four events: sit and reach, push-ups, sit-ups, and either a 1.5-mile run or a 500-yard

[14] U.S. Army, undated (a).

[15] See Pringle, 2011.

[16] NROTC, 2011b.

[17] NROTC, 2011a.

swim) with a "good-low" rating in each category. This means that a man (17–19 years old) needs to be able to complete the sit and reach, 51 push-ups, and 62 sit-ups in two minutes each and a 1.5-mile run in 11 minutes or a 500-yard swim in 11 minutes and 15 seconds; a woman (17–19 years old) needs to be able to complete the sit and reach, 24 push-ups, and 62 sit-ups in two minutes each and a 1.5-mile run in 13 minutes and 30 seconds or a 500-yard swim in 13 minutes.[18] Two-year scholarship applicants are not required to submit SAT exam or ACT scores. Instead, the applicant must have a minimum college GPA of 2.5 and must have passed the Navy PRT with a good-low rating in each category. Enlisted sailors can apply to NROTC through the Seaman to Admiral-21 Commissioning Program. To be eligible for this program, an applicant must score a minimum of 1,000 on the SAT exam (verbal and math) or a 41 (composite score) on the ACT. He or she must have also passed a recent Navy PRT with a good-low rating in each category.

Like they do for the other services, selection boards review and select applicants for scholarship awards based on a whole-person concept. Our research could not find more information on the other factors considered during selection, the weighting of each factor, or specifics of the selection process. In addition, we are not aware of the requirements for nonscholarship applicants.

The Marine Corps option for joining NROTC has similar requirements. To be eligible, a scholarship applicant must score a minimum of either 1,000 on the SAT exam (math and critical reading), a 22 on the ACT (average of math and English), or an AFQT score of 74. The AFQT is a composite score covering four subtests of the ASVAB: word knowledge, paragraph comprehension, arithmetic reasoning, and mathematical knowledge. Applicants must also take the Marine Corps PFT, which includes pull-ups, sit-ups, and a three-mile run. There is no minimum score required on the physical fitness test for four-year scholarship applicants. However, a two-year scholarship applicant is required to have a score of 225 on the Marine Corps PFT. This can be obtained through any combination of points on the three events, with each event being worth a maximum of 100 points.[19] Semester and cumulative GPA in high school and college (for two-year scholarship applicants) and extracurricular activities are also taken into account during the scholarship selection process. Each nonscholarship applicant is also required to meet the same minimum score of either 1,000 on the SAT exam (math and critical reading), a 22 on the ACT (composite score), or an AFQT score of 74. Applicants must also take the Marine Corps PFT.

Like they do for the other services, selection boards review and select applicants based on a whole-person concept. Again, our research could not find more information on other factors considered during selection, the weighting of each factor, or specifics of the selection process.

Air Force. The Air Force ROTC (AFROTC) program operates at more than 1,100 colleges and universities (144 host programs and more than 1,025 cross-town partnerships).[20] It has been the largest commissioning source for the Air Force in recent years, composing roughly 37 to 41 percent of all officer accessions.[21] Like Army ROTC, the AFROTC program is broken down into two major courses: the general military course and the professional officer

[18] Chief of Naval Operations (OPNAV) Instruction 1532.1/Marine Corps Order (MCO) 1532.1, 2008.

[19] MCO 6100.12, 2002.

[20] AFROTC, undated (d).

[21] Office of the Under Secretary of Defense, 2010.

course. The general military course is taken during the freshman and sophomore years of college and does not require a service commitment for participation. Therefore, a student who is not on scholarship can also take the course to see whether AFROTC is something he or she would be interested in pursuing. The professional officer course is taken during the junior and senior years of college and requires a commitment to serve in the Air Force following graduation. In addition, all students who are not on scholarship must apply and be selected to enroll in the professional officer course.

As shown in Table 3.1, the Air Force uses the following standardized tests to determine eligibility for scholarship selection and enrollment into the professional officer course: SAT exam or ACT, Air Force PFT, and AFOQT.[22] College applicants for both three- and two-year scholarships and all applicants for the professional officer course (even those without a scholarship) must take and meet the minimum requirements for the AFOQT. The AFOQT has several subtests to assess math, verbal, and analytical skills, as well as to measure pilot and navigator potential. To be eligible for scholarship or enrollment into the professional officer course, an applicant must score at or above the 15th percentile on the verbal portion and at or above the 10th percentile on the quantitative portion of the AFOQT.[23] The AFOQT requirement can be waived if the applicant failed twice to meet this minimum requirement but possesses other outstanding qualities. Also, for enrollment in the AFROTC program, a graduating high school student applying for a four-year scholarship is allowed to submit SAT exam or ACT scores in place of the AFOQT if he or she has a minimum score of 1,100 (verbal and math) on the SAT exam or a 24 (composite score) on the ACT.[24] Nevertheless, if the applicant wants to qualify for the AFROTC scholarship, he or she still has to take the AFOQT and attain the minimum scores described here.[25]

All AFROTC scholarship applicants except high school seniors, and all applicants to the professional officer course (regardless of scholarship status) must also take the Air Force PFT (three events: push-ups, sit-ups, and a 1.5-mile run, plus a measure of abdominal circumference) and receive a minimum score of 75 (nonwaivable).[26] The 75-point total can be obtained through various score combinations in each of the events. To grant 75 points, the Air Force recommends that a man (less than 30 years old) be able to complete at least 44 push-ups and 46 sit-ups in one minute each, complete a 1.5-mile run in 12 minutes and 54 seconds, and have an abdominal circumference measurement of 37.5 inches; a woman (less than 30 years old) needs to be able to complete 27 push-ups and 42 sit-ups in one minute each, complete a 1.5-mile run in 15 minutes and 21 seconds, and have an abdominal circumference measurement of 34 inches. A four-year scholarship candidate graduating from high school is not required to meet a minimum score on the physical fitness test, but the score will be a factor in the scholarship selection decision.

Civilian scholarship selections are made using the whole-person concept through a board process that consists of a panel of three Air Force officers.[27] Scholarship candidates are rated

---

[22] AFROTC, undated (e).

[23] Hardison, Sims, and Wong, 2010; Ingerick, 2005.

[24] AFROTC, undated (a).

[25] AFROTC, undated (b), undated (c).

[26] AFROTC, undated (e).

[27] Ingerick, 2005.

on three factors: academics or aptitude, experience or leadership potential, and commitment to or fitness for military service. Candidates are scored by the board members on each factor and are then ranked to determine scholarship selection. At the time of this writing, however, we are not aware of the weight given to each factor.

There are also several ways in which active-duty enlisted applicants can join AFROTC, including options for AFROTC scholarships.[28] Applicants for these enlisted opportunities must meet the same requirements for the AFOQT and Air Force PFT, as well as the requirements for the SAT exam or ACT if they do not have any previously graded college work. The enlisted selection process is made using a board process that is similar to the one for officers.[29] Candidates are rated independently by three board members on three factors: academics or aptitude (35 percent), military performance or leadership potential (50 percent), and physical fitness (15 percent). Candidates are scored by the board members on each factor and are then ranked to determine eligibility to enroll in AFROTC (a total board score of 55 is required to be eligible).

All candidates to the professional officer course must also go through a selection process (scholarship or nonscholarship). Again, the board uses the whole-person concept to make decisions. There are four main selection factors: a relative standing score (which ranks students among their peers) (50 percent), college GPA (20 percent), Air Force PFT score (15 percent), and AFOQT score (15 percent).[30] Candidates are then ranked on an order of merit list (OML) using their total score from these four factors. The top students are offered admission to the course. The cutoff for the number of students accepted is determined mainly by Air Force strength requirements.

Officer Candidate School and Officer Training School

A second major source of newly commissioned officers is OCS (as it is known in the Army, Navy, Marine Corps, and Coast Guard) or OTS (for the Air Force). OCS is the largest officer commissioning source for the Marine Corps.[31] An applicant to OCS or OTS can be an active-duty enlisted member with a recommendation from his or her commanding officer, or he or she can be a non–prior service, college graduate civilian.[32] At a minimum, each OCS or OTS applicant must be a college senior or have a bachelor's degree, be a U.S. citizen, and be at least 18 (or, for the Navy, 19) years of age at the time of enrollment.[33]

Where standardized tests are concerned, our research indicates that the services use the tests shown in Table 3.2 to determine eligibility of applicants and to make selection decisions. Our research finds that all the services use standardized tests as a factor for selecting applicants into their OCS and OTS programs. All the services also use the whole-person concept, in which aptitude tests and physical fitness test scores are combined with other factors, as well

---

[28] Air University, 2008.

[29] Ingerick, 2005.

[30] Ingerick, 2005.

[31] U.S. Marine Corps, undated (a).

[32] Again, direct commissioned officers enter OCS or OTS for basic officer leadership training after they are given their commissions, and they are not covered in this discussion.

[33] Army Regulation (AR) 350-51, 2001; U.S. Navy, undated (b); U.S. Marine Corps, undated (a); Air University, undated (a).

Table 3.2
Tests for Applicants to Officer Candidate School and Officer Training School

Test	Army	Navy	Air Force	Marine Corps	Coast Guard
ACT	x			x	x
AFOQT			x		
Air Force PFT			x		
APFT	x				
ASTB		x		x	
ASVAB	x			x	x
CLEP	x				x
ECLT or ALCPT	x		x		
LSAT				x	
Marine Corps PFT				x	
Navy PRT		x			
SAT exam	x			x	x

NOTE: ASTB = Aviation Selection Test Battery. CLEP = College-Level Examination Program; "CLEP" and "College-Level Examination Program" are registered trademarks of the College Board. ECLT = English Comprehension Level Test. ALCPT = American Language Course Placement Test. LSAT = Law School Admission Test.

as the judgment of board members regarding other candidate measures of merit (e.g., informal standards on the aptitude and fitness tests might actually be much higher than the stated requirement). Within this process, some tests can be used solely as cutoffs, whereas, for others, a competitive score might be higher than the actual cutoff. However, our research suggests that this usage is not official and that selection boards enjoy considerable discretion in evaluating applicants. We also did not generally find options for waivers or other substitutes for these standardized tests and their minimum score requirements. Brief descriptions for each test and how the services use them are provided in the sections that follow.

Army. Army OCS, located at Fort Benning, Georgia, is officially the 3rd Battalion, 11th Infantry Regiment, which is a subunit of the U.S. Army Infantry School.[34] OCS consists of a 12-week instruction program in which candidates participate in classroom and field training designed to develop them into leaders for the Army.

As shown in Table 3.2, the Army uses the following standardized tests to determine eligibility and selection for enrollment into Army OCS: ACT, APFT, ASVAB, CLEP, ECLT or ALCPT, and SAT exam.[35] The ACT or SAT exam is required of enlisted soldiers.[36] Each of these applicants must score a minimum of 19 (composite score) on the ACT or 850 (verbal and math) on the SAT exam, and the scores must be dated within six years of his or her application

[34] U.S. Army, undated (c).

[35] AR 350-51, 2001.

[36] A four-year college degree is a basic requirement for commissioning, so an OCS candidate without a four-year college degree must have completed at least 90 semester hours toward a college degree and must complete the bachelor's program within one year of his or her application to OCS.

to OCS. A civilian applicant must hold a four-year college degree and is not required to submit ACT or SAT exam scores. An applicant whose primary language is not English must also pass the ECLT or ALCPT with a score of 80 or higher. Every applicant, active-duty enlisted or college graduate civilian, must score 110 or higher on the GT section of the ASVAB. Finally, every applicant must also pass the APFT with a minimum total of 180 points (60 points minimum for each of the three events). Test scores needed in order to be a competitive candidate can be higher than these official cutoff scores, particularly on the APFT. Candidates for some postcollege commissioning programs who do not have bachelor's degrees can submit results on CLEP subject-area tests toward the number of required semester-hours. There are several different types of exams that can be used for this purpose. However, these scores are not directly submitted to the services; these tests must be listed on a college transcript as having entitled the student to credits at that school.[37]

Separate boards review and select college graduate civilian and active-duty enlisted applicants, and each has its own slots for admission to the Army OCS. U.S. Army Recruiting Command organizes the selection board for college graduate civilians; the U.S. Army Human Resources Command organizes the selection board for active-duty enlisted applicants. At the time of this writing, we are not aware of what other factors are included as part of the OCS selection process or how each factor is weighted in the selection process.

Navy. The Navy OCS is located at Naval Station Newport, Rhode Island, and is overseen by the Naval Service Training Command.[38] Like the Army OCS program, it consists of a 12-week course in which candidates learn about the Navy and are trained to become future leaders. College graduate civilians and active-duty enlisted personnel can both apply to OCS, with the former making up about 75 percent of all candidate officers. Every application by an active-duty enlisted member must be accompanied by a nomination from the applicant's commanding officer.

As shown in Table 3.2, the Navy uses only two standardized tests for preliminary screening into OCS: the Officer Aptitude Rating (OAR), which is a composite of the ASTB, and the Navy PRT. These are taken before selection into the program and are used as part of a whole-person concept to select applicants for OCS. Other factors considered include college GPA, employment experiences, physical examination results, and extracurricular activities. Unlike applicants to Army OCS, every applicant to Navy OCS—college graduate civilians and active-duty enlisted alike—must hold a four-year college degree at the time of application. Neither the SAT exam nor ACT is required. An applicant must score a minimum of 35 points on the OAR in order to be qualified for selection into OCS. The OAR is the combined score for three sections of the ASTB (mathematics, reading, and mechanical comprehension).[39] As for the Navy PRT, although it is not a required component of the initial application package, an applicant must take the Navy PRT after he or she has completed the medical examination. Civilian applicants must have a "satisfactory-medium" score to be eligible for selection. This means that a man (20 to 24 years old) must be able to complete a minimum of 50 sit-ups and 42 push-ups within two minutes each and complete a 1.5-mile run in no more than 13 minutes

---

[37] Fort Bragg, undated.

[38] Naval Education and Training Command, 2010.

[39] Our research indicates that racial/ethnic minorities who score "below the cuff" (minimum qualifications for entry) can be accepted at the Army Preparatory School before being placed in OCS.

and 15 seconds or swim 500 yards in 12 minutes and 15 seconds; a woman (20 to 24 years old) must be able to complete a minimum of 50 sit-ups and 17 push-ups within two minutes each and complete a 1.5-mile run in no more than 15 minutes and 15 seconds or swim 500 yards in 14 minutes. Active-duty enlisted applicants must meet higher standards in the Navy PRT than civilian applicants must. An enlisted applicant must have at least a "good-low" score. At the time of this writing, we are not aware of what other factors are included as part of the OCS selection process or how each factor is weighted in the selection process.

Air Force. The Air Force OTS program is located in Montgomery, Alabama, at Maxwell Air Force Base and operates under the Air Education and Training Command.[40] Classes last about 13.5 weeks, and a new class begins about every six weeks. As is true for the Navy OCS program, a civilian or active-duty enlisted applicant to OTS must hold at least a four-year college degree at the time of the application. OTS organizes its own selection boards, each made up of five colonels, to review all applications. There are different boards for rated and nonrated applicants. Rated jobs in the Air Force consist of pilots (including pilots of remotely piloted aircraft), combat-system officers (navigators), and air battle managers; all other specialties are considered nonrated jobs. OTS selection boards can occur as frequently as once every six weeks in alignment with the class schedules, but typically, there are two rated and two nonrated OTS boards annually.

As shown in Table 3.2, the main standardized tests used by the Air Force are the AFOQT, the Air Force PFT, and the ECLT (for applicants whose primary language is not English). In determining selection into OTS, selection board members (five total) use the whole-person concept to independently rate each candidate using a 1–10 scale for each of three factors: education or aptitude, experience, and potential or adaptability.[41] The education or aptitude factor includes the applicant's academic discipline, college GPA and transcripts, and AFOQT score. The experience factor includes past employment, letters of recommendation, awards and honors, community service, athletics and hobbies, military experience, and scope or level of leadership responsibility. For an active-duty enlisted applicant, this includes his or her performance reports and recommendations from his or her commanding officer. The potential or adaptability factor includes reports of initial interviews with the applicant, conducted by officers of the Air Force Recruiting Service (AFRS); letters of recommendation; assessment of the applicant's communication skills; and any law violations. If board members' ratings differ by more than 1.5 points, the applicants must be rescored until the discrepancy is resolved. Each factor is worth one-third of the total score for each panel member, with panel members' scores summed to get a total board score. An applicant who receives a board score of 30 or more points is then ranked into an OML and selected on the basis of quality and career field strength requirements.

Where standardized tests are concerned, the AFOQT is the only test that every applicant is required to take as part of his or her initial application. (The ECLT is required only of those applicants whose primary language is not English. They must also sit for an interview at the Defense Language Institute Foreign Language Center.) For the AFOQT, the applicant needs to score at or above the 10th percentile in the math section and at or above the 15th percentile on the verbal section to be competitive. The Air Force PFT is then given before attending OTS.

---

[40] Air University, undated (b).

[41] Ingerick, 2005.

Marine Corps. Marine Corps OCS is located at Marine Corps Base Quantico, Virginia, and operates under the Marine Corps Recruiting Command.[42] The OCS program is the largest producer of commissioned officers for the Marine Corps, with only a small number of its officers coming from the U.S. Naval Academy (USNA) and the NROTC program. An applicant who has already completed his or her bachelor's degree can participate in a ten-week Officer Candidate Course (OCC), which runs three times per year. An applicant still in college can participate in the Platoon Leaders Class (PLC). College freshmen and sophomores must complete two six-week summer training sessions in the space of two years, while juniors attend one ten-week summer training session. An applicant can be an active-duty enlisted member or a civilian with no prior military experience.

Applicants go through three phases in the application process. First, the applicant sits through an interview and initial screening by a recruiter. Second, the applicant undergoes a physical examination, background check, and mental and moral evaluation. Third, the selection board reviews the application. As shown in Table 3.2, the Marine Corps uses the following standardized tests to determine eligibility and selection for enrollment into its OCS programs: ACT, ASTB, ASVAB, LSAT, Marine Corps PFT, and SAT exam.

Applicants for OCC must have completed a four-year college degree by the time they enroll. A civilian college senior who does not yet have a college degree at the time of application must submit SAT exam (minimum score of 1,000 for combined verbal and math sections) or ACT (minimum 22 for math and English average) scores, while an active-duty enlisted applicant can submit an AFQT score in place of an SAT exam or ACT score.[43] A minimum AFQT score of 74 is required.

As is true for college seniors applying to OCC, an applicant to the PLC must submit his or her SAT exam (minimum score of 1,000 for combined verbal and math sections), ACT (minimum 22 for math and English average) scores, or the AFQT score in place of SAT exam and ACT scores (a minimum AFQT score of 74 is required).[44]

Applicants for both of these OCS programs are also required to choose to join one of three fields—ground, air, or law—and a few standardized tests are used to assess potential for training. Those who seek to become pilots or naval flight officers must take the Navy or Marine Corps ASTB and be medically qualified for flight training. An applicant who seeks to become a staff judge advocate must have a minimum score of 150 on the LSAT.[45] He or she must also be enrolled in a law program during the OCS training and must pass the bar exam before he or she can proceed to TBS, a six-month leadership training program that every newly commissioned officer must complete after the OCS program and before obtaining his or her Marine Corps military occupational specialty (MOS). Finally, each applicant must pass the Marine Corps PFT with a combined score of 225 or better for three events (sit-ups, push-ups, and a three-mile run or a 500-yard swim).

---

[42] U.S. Marine Corps, undated (a).

[43] "The Few, the Proud, the Marines," undated.

[44] U.S. Marine Corps, undated (c); "Officer Commissioning Programs for College Freshman [sic] Through Juniors," undated.

[45] All other services use LSAT scores for applicants in the law profession, but these individuals are law school graduates and usually directly commissioned into the judge advocate general corps.

Selection boards meet several times per year and use a host of factors, including academic performance, physical fitness, character, extracurricular activities, and work experience, in their selection decisions. At the time of this writing, however, we are not aware of how each of these factors is weighted in the selection process.

Coast Guard. The Coast Guard OCS is located at the USCGA in New London, Connecticut.[46] Its OCS program, at 17 weeks in length, is the longest of all the five services' OCS programs. Graduates gain commissions as ensigns in the Coast Guard. After the USCGA, OCS is the second-largest commissioning source for the Coast Guard.[47] Applicants can be civilians with no prior military experience, or they can be active-duty enlisted personnel.

The Coast Guard requires any civilian applicant to hold a four-year college degree to enroll in OCS but does not require this from active-duty enlisted applicants.[48] As shown in Table 3.2, the Coast Guard uses the following standardized tests to determine eligibility and selection for enrollment into OCS: ACT, ASVAB, CLEP, and SAT exam.

An applicant with a four-year college degree submits his or her GPA as part of the application package, while an applicant without a four-year college degree can submit his or her ACT, SAT exam, or ASVAB scores. For the ACT, the applicant must have a minimum composite score of 23. For the SAT exam, the minimum requirement is a combined total of 1,100 for the math and verbal sections. For the ASVAB, a GT score of 109 is required. In addition, the Coast Guard has a category of temporary commission applicants for active-duty enlisted personnel at E-5 rank and above with at least four years of active-duty service in any of the services. Each of these applicants should ideally have completed a four-year college degree. Any applicant who has not done so must have "25th percentile scores on general CLEP exams" (we do not have any further detailed information on the specific subject tests required)

> or have completed at least one year of college (30 semester[-hours] or 45 quarter hours) at an accredited college or university. [Each] Temporary Commission [applicant] must also have completed one college-level math class or [have passed] the general math CLEP exam.[49]

At the time of this writing, we are not aware of what other factors are included as part of the OCS selection process or how each factor is weighted in the selection process.

Service Academies

The Army, Navy, Air Force, and Coast Guard each has a service academy that provides enrollees with a four-year college education and leadership training to prepare them to become commissioned officers in the armed forces. Almost all applicants are high school seniors; a few are active-duty enlisted personnel. The Army, Navy, and Air Force academies each admits between 1,250 to 1,400 cadets and midshipmen each year.[50] In the past, each has produced about 800 to 1,000 graduates annually.[51] However, enrollment at the service academies is now

---

[46] U.S. Coast Guard Academy, undated (d).

[47] U.S. Coast Guard, undated (a).

[48] U.S. Coast Guard Training Center, 2010.

[49] U.S. Coast Guard Academy, undated (d).

[50] U.S. Military Academy at West Point, undated (b); U.S. Naval Academy, undated (b).

[51] Office of the Under Secretary of Defense, 2010.

being reduced with the impending force reductions. The USCGA is the smallest of the service academies, with new enrollments of about 300 per year and about 200 graduates annually.[52]

The service academies all use similar requirements to determine eligibility of applicants and the same whole-person approach to selection. At a minimum, every service academy applicant must be a U.S. citizen, unmarried with no dependents, and be at least 17 to 23 years of age at the time of enrollment. Each applicant to a service academy other than the USCGA must also receive a nomination to the academy, usually from a member of the U.S. House of Representatives or U.S. Senate or the President or Vice President of the United States. Whole-person score assessments tend to cover three dimensions: academic, leadership or character, and physical fitness. As with other whole-person assessments, the boards are permitted to adjust scores up or down based on their holistic assessment.

Where standardized tests are concerned, our research indicates that the services use the standardized tests shown in Table 3.3 to determine eligibility and final selection of applicants. Like other colleges and universities do, the service academies rely on ACT and SAT exam scores. All DoD service academies other than the USCGA also require the same physical fitness assessment, the Candidate Fitness Assessment (CFA), which has six events (basketball throw; cadence pull-ups or, for women, flexed-arm hang; a shuttle run; sit-ups; push-ups; and a one-mile run), each with a minimum passing score.[53] Brief descriptions of each test and how the services use them are provided in the sections that follow.

Army. The U.S. Military Academy at West Point (USMA) is located in West Point, New York.[54] As Table 3.3 shows, the main standardized tests required for admission are the SAT exam, ACT, and CFA. Selection into USMA is based on whether the applicant both is qualified and received a nomination to attend the academy. To qualify for admission, an applicant must pass the CFA, meet medical standards, and have a recommendation from the academic board as being qualified. The recommendation from the academic board is based on a whole-person score, which is composed of several different factors, including standardized test scores.

There are three main factors that compose the whole-person score: academics, leadership, and physical fitness. The academic portion, which includes high school GPA, class rank, and SAT exam or ACT scores, represents roughly 60 percent of the total score. The leadership por-

Table 3.3
Tests for Service Academy Applicants

Test	Army	Navy	Air Force	Coast Guard
ACT	x	x	x	x
CFA	x	x	x	
Coast Guard PFE				x
SAT exam	x	x	x	x

NOTE: PFE = physical fitness exam.

---

[52] U.S. Coast Guard, 2010; Grogan, 2010.

[53] U.S. Merchant Marine Academy, undated.

[54] U.S. Military Academy at West Point, undated (a).

tion comprises roughly 30 percent of the score and is determined based on leadership qualities and positions the individual has held, such as being a class officer or a sports team captain.

Finally, the physical fitness portion comprises 10 percent of the score and is predominantly made up of the applicant's score on the CFA, but it also includes other evidence of athletic ability, such as being on a sports team in high school.

Navy. USNA, located in Annapolis, Maryland, produces officers for both the Navy and the Marine Corps.[55] (The Marine Corps does not have an academy of its own. Midshipmen at USNA can choose to join the Marine Corps, and the number selected annually is based on an agreement between the Navy and the Marine Corps.[56]) As Table 3.3 shows, the main standardized tests required for admission are the SAT exam or ACT and the CFA. As is the case with USMA, admission into USNA is based on whether the applicant both is qualified and received a nomination to attend the academy. To qualify for admission, an applicant must pass the CFA, meet medical standards, and have a recommendation from the admission board as being qualified. The recommendation from the admission board is based on a whole-person score or multiple, which is composed of several different factors, including standardized test scores.

As is the case at the other service academies, there are three main factors that compose the whole-person score at USNA: academics, leadership, and physical fitness. The academic factor includes high school GPA, class rank, and SAT exam or ACT scores. The ACT or SAT exam scores account for roughly one-third of the final whole-person score, with the quantitative score being worth roughly twice the verbal score. A candidate's highest verbal and highest quantitative scores from the SAT exam and ACT are used. The leadership portion is determined based on leadership qualities and positions the individual has held, such as being a class officer or a sports team captain. The physical fitness portion is predominantly made up of the applicant's score on the CFA, but it also includes other evidence of athletic ability, such as being on a sports team in high school. At the time of this writing, we are not aware of the exact weight given to each of these factors in determining the whole-person multiple. A candidate can also have extra points added to his or her scores for participation in several areas, such as being a science, technology, engineering, or math major; being an Eagle Scout; or attending a magnet school.

Air Force. The U.S. Air Force Academy (USAFA) is located north of Colorado Springs, Colorado.[57] As Table 3.3 shows, the main standardized tests required for admission are the SAT exam or ACT and the CFA. Selection into USAFA is consistent with selection at the other academies and is based on whether the applicant both is qualified and received a nomination to attend the academy. To qualify for admission, an applicant must pass the CFA, meet medical standards, and have a recommendation from the academic board as being qualified. The recommendation from the academic board is based on a whole-person score, which is composed of several different factors, including standardized test scores.

There are three main factors that compose the whole-person score: academics, leadership, and a selection panel rating. The academic portion, which includes high school GPA, class

---

[55] USNA, undated (a).

[56] In recent years, increased demand for junior Marine Corps officers has resulted in a higher number of Naval Academy graduates gaining commissions in the Marine Corps. Of the graduating class of 2009, more than 25 percent joined the Marine Corps, the highest percentage ever. See Halsey, 2009.

[57] U.S. Air Force Academy, undated (b).

rank, and SAT exam or ACT scores, comprises roughly 60 percent of the total score. The leadership portion comprises roughly 20 percent of the score and is determined based on leadership qualities and positions the individual has held, such as being a class officer or a sports team captain. Finally, the selection panel rating comprises 20 percent of the score and is composed of the applicant's score on the CFA, as well as a rating by the academy's liaison officer after conducting an interview with the candidate.

Coast Guard. The USCGA is in New London, Connecticut.[58] The USCGA, like the other academies, uses a whole-person approach to selection. Requirements include submission of evaluations from an applicant's high school teachers of math, English, and physical education (or coach) or, if the applicant is active-duty enlisted, an evaluation from his or her commanding officer. High school grades, too, are reviewed. As Table 3.3 shows, the main standardized tests required for admission are the SAT exam or ACT and the Coast Guard PFE. The USCGA, like its counterpart institutions for other services, does not specify any minimum score for the SAT exam or ACT but recommends a score of 1,100 on the SAT exam (combined verbal and math) or 24 (composite score) on the ACT to be competitive.[59] For the Coast Guard PFE, the applicant must score at least a combined 130 points for three events: push-ups, sit-ups, and a 1.5-mile run.[60] Each event is worth up to 100 points, with no minimum score required for each individual event—only a combined total score. The Coast Guard reports that, on average, men complete 36 push-ups and 78 sit-ups in two minutes each and complete the 1.5-mile run in 10 minutes and 17 seconds, and women complete 22 push-ups and 71 sit-ups in two minutes each and complete the 1.5-mile run in 12 minutes. These average scores add up to more than 130 points. At the time of this writing, we are not aware of how the selection process for admission into USCGA works or all the factors considered as part of the admission decision.

Branch, Specialty, or Job Selection

A key part of this research is to examine the role of standardized tests in selection into key career fields in the services. For the purposes of this research, a *key career field* is defined as a career that tends to produce the most flag officers (grades O-7 to O-10). In general, research has found that those career fields most associated with the mission of the particular branch of service are those that also produce the most flag officers. For example, in the Air Force, the majority of flag officers are pilots; in the Army and Marine Corps, the majority of flag officers are from the combat arms career fields; in the Navy, the majority of flag officers are from the unrestricted line (URL) communities (the surface warfare, aviation, submarine warfare, naval special warfare, and explosive ordnance disposal [EOD] communities).[61] For at least the Marine Corps and the Navy, these also happen to be the largest career fields and communities, with the majority of lower-ranking officers belonging to these career fields.[62] Only the Coast

---

[58] USCGA, undated (a).

[59] USCGA, undated (b).

[60] USCGA, 2010.

[61] Lim et al., 2009; "Military Occupations and Implications for Racial/Ethnic and Gender Diversity," 2010.

[62] "Military Occupations and Implications for Racial/Ethnic and Gender Diversity," 2010.

Guard has a more even distribution across career fields, with no single career field producing a far higher percentage of its flag officers.

Overall, the information we collected suggests that aviation is the main branch, specialty, or job assignment that requires additional standardized tests. Considering that pilots produce the most flag officers for the Air Force, the use of standardized tests is thus likely to have the largest impact on key career fields for the Air Force. However, to make empirically based determinations, we need data for all services.

In general, all services and commissioning sources make branch, specialty, or job selections in a similar manner. Specifically, all individuals are allowed to submit their rank-ordered preferences for career fields. The extent to which an individual receives one of his or her first choices depends on where he or she ranks on the commissioning source OML. The OML ranks students based on several factors, but it usually includes academics, leadership, and physical fitness. In the next section are more details on this process for each source and service, as well as an overview of the standardized tests used by each commissioning program for branch, specialty, or job selection.

ROTC

In ROTC, branch, specialty, or job selection generally happens during the junior year of college. The overall process across services is somewhat similar in that the candidate is allowed to submit his or her own career field preferences and is then ultimately assigned a career field based on preferences and where he or she ranks in an overall OML. With the exception of aviation, most career fields do not require any additional testing—only that the candidate meet the necessary physical and medical requirements. Table 3.4 presents the standardized tests used for branch, specialty, or job selection in ROTC. Brief descriptions for each test and how the services use them are provided in the sections that follow.

Army. In the Army, the branch selection process occurs in the junior year of college. Branch selection is primarily based on individual branch preference and a national order of merit score (OMS).[63] The OMS is based on three components, with a maximum of 100 points.

Table 3.4
Tests and Branch, Specialty, or Job Selection in ROTC

Test	Army	Navy	Air Force	Marine Corps
AFAST	x			
AFOQT			x	
Air Force PFT			x	
APFT	x			
ASTB		x		x
TBAS			x	
TBS-specific standardized tests				x

NOTE: The Coast Guard is not covered in this section because it does not have a ROTC program. AFAST = Alternate Flight Aptitude Selection Test. TBAS = Test of Basic Aviation Skills.

---

[63] U.S. Army ROTC, undated (b).

The first component is GPA, which is worth a total of 40 points. The second component is leadership (e.g., performance in leadership positions, extracurricular activities, accession OML, leadership evaluation), which is worth a total of 45 points. The last component is physical fitness, which covers the remaining 15 points (APFT score comprises 90 percent of this component). Bonus points are also awarded for specific accomplishments. Based on cadet preferences, the cadet's rank in the OML, and the number of slots available within each branch, an active-duty branching board places each cadet into the appropriate branch starting with the top of the list to the bottom, with the goal that each cadet will get one of his or her top three choices.

Aviation candidates are the only cadets who must meet additional requirements to be eligible for selection. Specifically, an aviation candidate must pass a flight physical and have a minimum score of 90 on the AFAST. The AFAST consists of seven subtests to assess aviation-related knowledge. AFAST scores, along with other factors (e.g., academic qualifications and flight experience), are then used to select candidates. At the time of this writing, we do not have more information on the other factors or their weights in the selection decision.

Navy. The community selection process for NROTC takes place during the beginning of the senior year of college. Each midshipman submits a service selection package in August of his or her senior year of college. As part of this package, the midshipman ranks his or her top choices, of which he or she is required to select three URL designators (i.e., surface warfare, aviation, submarine warfare, naval special warfare, EOD community) and one restricted line (RL) (for those not eligible to command at sea) or staff corps designator. The midshipman is then given an OMS, which is calculated separately for aviators and nonaviators, due to additional aviator requirements. Specifically, aviation candidates are also required to take the ASTB and must meet minimum score cutoffs to qualify. Each aviation candidate must receive a 4 on the Academic Qualifications Rating (AQR) and a 5 on either the Pilot Flight Aptitude Rating (PFAR) or Flight Officer Flight Aptitude Rating (FOFAR), depending on whether the candidate would like to be a pilot or a flight officer. For nonaviation candidates, the OMS is based on cumulative GPA (45 percent), aptitude (35 percent), academic major (10 percent), and rating from the professor of naval science (PNS) (the commanding officer in charge of courses) (10 percent). For aviation candidates, the OMS is based on cumulative GPA (27 percent), aptitude (21 percent), academic major (6 percent), PNS rating (6 percent), the ASTB AQR (15 percent), and the ASTB PFAR or FOFAR (25 percent). A service assignment panel then rank-orders the midshipman based on his or her OMS score and gives assignments based on the midshipman's ranking and preferences and Navy manpower requirements.

Air Force. In the Air Force, there are two separate branching processes: one for rated line officers and one for nonrated line officers. Rated line officers make up the aviation side of the Air Force and consist of pilots (including pilots of remotely piloted aircraft), combat system officers, and air battle managers, while nonrated line officers comprise the remaining specialties. For nonrated line officers, the specialty selection process begins in the junior year of AFROTC. AFROTC detachment commanders submit what is called *Form 53* for each cadet, detailing academic major, coursework, skills in a foreign language, six cadet-ranked specialty preferences, GPA, and AFROTC detachment ranking. This information is used to create a national OML to rank cadets. The Air Force then uses a computer algorithm to assign cadets to specialties based on manpower requirements, cadet preferences, and cadets' ranking on the OML. We could not obtain details on this algorithm and selection process.

Rated line officers must go through a selection board process to qualify for aviation training. Like those seeking other aviation careers in the services, rated line officers must take additional standardized tests to qualify. Specifically, aviation candidates are selected using the Pilot Candidate Selection Method (PCSM) score.[64] The PCSM is composed of the AFOQT pilot composite score, the TBAS score, and flying hours. The TBAS is a computerized psychomotor test. We are not aware of the minimums or weights for these tests in computing the PCSM score, however. The PCSM score counts as 15 percent in the overall OMS received by the aviation applicant. The remaining factors are the applicant's cumulative GPA (15 percent), most recent Air Force PFT score (10 percent), unit commander's ranking or relative standing score (50 percent), and field training score (10 percent). Together, these factors determine an individual's rank on the national OML. Applicants are chosen starting with the top of the list until all slots are filled, with AFROTC annually allocated a specific number of pilot slots.

Marine Corps. A student enrolled in NROTC and seeking a commission in the Marine Corps chooses his or her MOS during TBS. The student is commissioned as a second lieutenant at the end of NROTC training and before enrolling in TBS for six months of leadership training. At the end of training, each officer submits his or her MOS preferences. To determine MOS assignment, the officer is given a performance ranking based only on his or her performance in TBS. Three factors are used to calculate a performance score: academics (32 percent), military skills (32 percent), and leadership (36 percent). The academic factor is a weighted average of ten standardized tests that the officer must complete while he or she is at TBS. Similarly, the military skill factor is a weighted average of 15 different military skill tests. Finally, the leadership factor is a weighted average of two leadership evaluation scores. Marine second lieutenants must achieve a 75-percent average in each of these categories and a 75-percent average overall in order to graduate from TBS. Each of these newly commissioned officers is then assigned to an MOS based on his or her preference. However, for each career field, only one-third of the assigned slots can come from the top third of the performance distribution, one-third from the middle, and one-third from the bottom.[65] Starting at the top of the distribution, candidates are given their first preference until all slots are filled.

Like candidates for the other services, aviation candidates are required to meet additional standards in order to be eligible. Generally, second lieutenants who are interested in aviation have already been selected and guaranteed an aviation contract prior to attending TBS, however. This process begins during the first few weeks of the program of instruction (in this case, NROTC), when individuals interested in aviation take the ASTB to see whether they qualify. The officer must receive at least a 4 on the AQR and at least a 6 on either the PFAR or FOFAR, depending on whether he or she would like to be a pilot or a flight officer.

Officer Candidate School and Officer Training School
Like we found for ROTC, we found that, for OCS and OTS, it is only for the aviation branch, specialty, or job selection that the services all use standardized aviation-specific aptitude tests to assess the potential of applicants for training. Further, test scores for these aviation aptitude tests, such as the AFAST and ASTB, are the primary determinants for selection. For the Navy, Air Force, and Marine Corps, an applicant to OCS or OTS has to declare his or her branch, specialty, or job preference at the time of application. The candidate's preferred option, along with other factors, is part of his or her application package submitted to service selection

---

[64] PCSM, undated (b).

[65] Navy Judge Advocate General's Corps candidates are an exception to this: Although they attend TBS, they are already assigned to this branch upon enrollment into OCS.

boards for a whole-person review. However, we were not able to find detailed information on how standardized tests are used as part of the whole-person review. Table 3.5 shows tests for branch, specialty, or job selection at various service OCS and OTS programs. Brief descriptions for each test and how the services use it can be found in the sections that follow.

Army. An applicant to Army OCS can state his or her preferred branches at the time of application. Our research indicates that standardized test scores are used for selection only of those candidate officers who want to become pilots. Each of these candidate officers must obtain a score of 90 or higher on the AFAST.

Navy. For branch, specialty, or job selection purposes, the Navy and Marine Corps ASTB is used in one of two ways to assess the aptitude of officer candidates. A candidate seeking a nonaviation job need only to derive his or her OAR score from three of the Navy and Marine Corps ASTB subtests: math skills, reading comprehension, and mechanical comprehension. This score is then used as part of the whole-person score. Those seeking careers in aviation have to take all six subtests in the Navy and Marine Corps ASTB and must obtain minimum scores on the ASTB to qualify. Specifically, each candidate must receive at least a 4 on the AQR and at least a 5 on either the PFAR or FOFAR to qualify for training to become a pilot or flight officer.

Air Force. Officer candidates at Air Force OTS can apply to join one of three career fields: pilot or navigator, technical (and subtechnical), and nontechnical. The primary selection factors for selection to become a pilot or a navigator are college GPA and pilot or navigator composite scores on the AFOQT. Applicants to become pilots are also required to take the TBAS. Their AFOQT pilot composite score, TBAS score, and number of flying hours are used to produce the PCSM score. The PCSM score is submitted to the pilot selection board for review, along with other whole-person concept information, for evaluation and selection.

Marine Corps. For the Marine Corps OCS program, career field selection begins from the point of application to OCS, when applicants have to choose one of three fields (ground, air, or law). For those who seek careers as pilots and naval flight officers, their performance on the Navy or Marine Corps ASTB is the most critical selection factor. Each candidate must receive at least a 4 on the AQR and at least a 6 on either the PFAR or FOFAR, depending on whether he or she would like to be a pilot or a flight officer. A candidate who seeks to become a staff judge advocate must have a minimum score of 150 on the LSAT and be enrolled in a law program during OCS in addition to meeting medical and other training requirements. Judge advocate candidates must also pass the bar exam before they can proceed to TBS.

Table 3.5
Tests and Branch, Specialty, or Job Selection at Officer Candidate School and Officer Training School

Test	Army	Navy	Air Force	Marine Corps	Coast Guard
AFAST	x				
AFOQT			x		
ASVAB	x				
LSAT				x	
ASTB		x		x	x
TBAS			x		

For those second lieutenants without aviation or law contracts, MOS selection occurs during TBS when officers submit their MOS preferences at the end of this six-month training period. They go through the same process described for NROTC along with newly commissioned officers from NROTC and USNA.

Coast Guard. Coast Guard aviation candidates must also take the ASTB to qualify for aviation careers. Like Navy aviation candidates, a Coast Guard aviation candidate must receive at least a 4 on the AQR and at least a 5 on the PFAR or FOFAR, depending on his or her desire to be a pilot or flight officer.

Service Academies

Although the service academies are quite similar in their requirements and approaches to selecting applicants for enrollment, there is divergence in how they select cadets and midshipmen for branch, specialty, or job assignments. There are also some similarities, however, with how selection is done in ROTC programs, which, too, are four-year college and military leadership training programs. Again, aviation is the primary branch, specialty, or job that requires additional standardized tests. However, as was true for the other commissioning sources, we were not able to find detailed information on how these standardized tests are used as part of the selection system. Table 3.6 shows those standardized tests that are used for branch, specialty, or job selection at the service academies. Brief descriptions for each test and how each service uses it can be found in the sections that follow.

Army. At USMA, the branching process begins in November of the senior year. Each cadet is asked to rank his or her branch preferences, and each is assigned a Cadet Performance Rank (CPR). The CPR is based on a cadet's academic program score (55 percent), military program score (30 percent), and physical program score (15 percent).[66] The academic program score is the cadet's cumulative GPA. The cadet's military program score is the average of his or her grades in summer training, military duty performance, and military science. The physical program score is derived from the cadet's grades in his or her physical education courses, fitness test scores, and competitive athletic performance. Thus, the main standardized test used for every cadet is the cadet's fitness test—the APFT—which each cadet must take twice per year and meet the minimum performance standards by gender and age category. The AFAST is the only other standardized test required, but it is required only for those cadets who seek to become pilots. The applicant must have a score of 90 or higher to be eligible for selection.

Table 3.6
Tests and Branch, Specialty, or Job Selection at Service Academies

Test	Army	Navy	Marine Corps	Coast Guard
AFAST	x			
APFT	x			
ASTB		x	x	x
Specialized PFT		x		

NOTE: The Air Force is not included in this table because we are aware of no additional standardized tests that are required for Air Force specialty selection at USAFA.

[66] Lim et al., 2009.

Navy. Starting in the junior year at the academy, each midshipman is physically and medically screened to determine his or her qualification for the URL communities. As part of this screening, any midshipman who wishes to join aviation, the Navy SEALs (Sea, Air, and Land), or EOD is also required to pass additional standardized tests. In particular, aviation candidates must take and meet minimum scores on the ASTB. The candidate must receive an AQR score of 4 and a PFAR or FOFAR score of 5, depending on whether he or she seeks to become a pilot or a flight officer. SEAL and EOD candidates must pass a physical fitness screening test, which includes a 500-yard swim, push-ups, sit-ups, pull-ups, and 1.5-mile run (we do not have detailed information on the passing scores). These additional tests help to screen candidates and distinguish between qualified candidates in service assignment board reviews.

In the fall of the senior year, each USNA midshipman then submits six rank-ordered community preferences for only those communities in which he or she is qualified. Thus, only candidates who are physically qualified and have met the designated minimum scores on the ASTB are allowed to list aviation as a preference. Each midshipman is required to select from only the URL designators unless he or she is not physically qualified, at which point he or she can select an RL designator. Service assignment boards representing each occupational community (e.g., surface warfare, aviation) then do an initial screening of each applicant who picked their occupational community as his or her first choice. When the annual quota for the first choice of a midshipman is filled, his or her application is then reviewed by the board representing the occupational community of his or her second choice, third choice, and so forth. The service assignment boards select applicants based on a variety of factors, including academics, military performance, and summer training experience. Each board uses different factors and weights for these factors depending on the community it represents. As for standardized tests, both the ASTB and the physical fitness tests required during initial screening for aviation, the SEALs, and EOD can again be factored into final board decisions.

Air Force. For USAFA, each cadet submits his or her rank-ordered preferences for occupations and is then assigned based on these preferences and his or her OML ranking. The OML is determined by two panel boards of five officers who rate cadets on a 6–10 scale for their academic, military, and athletic performance.[67] Ratings from each board member are then summed for a total board score. These scores are then standardized, and the OML is created. Unlike graduates of the other services, USAFA graduates do not have to take an additional standardized test for selection into pilot training. Instead, cadets are selected based on their OML ranking. Thus, we found no additional standardized tests that were used during selection at USAFA.

Marine Corps. Upon graduation, Marine Corps officers who attended USNA will attend TBS, where MOS selection is determined. They will go through the same MOS assignment process as their peers from OCS and NROTC, as described previously.

Coast Guard. We do not have specific information on the assignment process for the Coast Guard. However, we do know that Coast Guard aviation candidates must also take the ASTB to qualify for aviation careers. Like Navy aviation candidates, each Coast Guard aviation candidate must receive an AQR score of 4 and a PFAR or FOFAR score of 5, depending on whether he or she would like to be a pilot or a flight officer.

---

[67] Lim et al., 2009.

Commissioning

The third key point outlined on our continuum is the commissioning stage, in which individuals enrolled in officer commissioning programs finally graduate and are commissioned as officers in the U.S. armed forces. As discussed in the previous sections, Army, Air Force, and Marine Corps officers are initially commissioned as second lieutenants (O-1); Navy and Coast Guard officers are initially commissioned as ensigns (O-1).

For all three of the commissioning sources discussed in the previous sections (ROTC, OCS/OTS, service academies), our research does not indicate the use of any standardized test scores other than physical fitness tests to determine officer candidate eligibility for commissioning. Each officer candidate is required to take service physical fitness tests for admission to the commissioning program and to take them on a regular basis during the program. All services have minimum performance requirements by gender and age for each event or in aggregate. This appears to be the only standardized test required for commissioning, however.

Promotion

The final key point outlined in our continuum is the promotion stage, which is critical to an officer's career advancement. Across the services, officer promotion is determined through a promotion board process, in which a panel of officers who are more senior reviews each candidate's qualifications and determines whether he or she should advance to the next rank. Our research indicates that none of the services explicitly requires any standardized tests to qualify for promotion. However, all of the services, either explicitly or implicitly, consider advanced education as a factor in their promotion decision. Although there are exceptions, most graduate programs require standardized test scores, such as the Graduate Record Examination (GRE) or the Graduate Management Admission Test (GMAT), to be submitted as part of the application process. Therefore, although these tests are outside of the direct control of DoD and are not required by DoD or the services, performance on these standardized tests can influence admission into programs for advanced degrees, the quality of programs to which officers are admitted, and their career prospects in the military. Additionally, passing physical fitness test scores are required for continuing in service, although waivers are available in some circumstances. Promotion boards have access to the physical fitness test scores of the officers they evaluate, but we could not obtain information on how that information is used.

CHAPTER FOUR

Conclusion

Overall, we found that standardized test scores are only one part of the military's holistic or whole-person approach to assessing individuals for entrance into officer commissioning programs and key career fields. Interviews, performance evaluations, GPA, and recommendations are also factored into final selection decisions and appointments. The whole-person approach also gives the selection board the ability to adjust scores based on its holistic view of the candidate. The types of standardized tests used also vary according to each decision point and by each service. Without data, we were unable to empirically examine the extent to which standardized tests affect selection decisions. However, according to the information available to us, standardized tests appear to play a major role in selection only for aviation careers in the services, not for other careers. Standardized tests also appear to play a smaller role in commissioning or promotion.

However, as the discussion in Chapter Three shows, our understanding of what and how standardized tests are used by the services requires additional information to fill current gaps. Most important is the fact that the way in which standardized tests function as part of a larger selection system is unclear in many cases. For many of these tests, we could not ascertain whether they are only used to screen out applicants (i.e., those who earn a score at or above a cutoff versus those who do not) or whether they are also used to select between two qualified candidates (i.e., both applicants have scores above the cutoff). In other cases, we could not determine how specific test scores are weighted as part of the broader selection system. For example, the TBAS is used as part of the PCSM score in pilot selection for the Air Force. However, we were not able to find published information on the weight it is given in calculating the PCSM score. We were also often not able to find published information on other factors that are used during the selection decision in addition to standardized test scores. Finally, we did not find complete information in many cases for whether tests could be waived, for whom, and under what circumstances.

This is likely due to a lack of publicly available information or published material on these selection processes and requirements. Having additional detailed information on the selection systems and how standardized tests are used would, therefore, be the first step toward determining the impact that standardized tests can have on selection decisions at various points in an officer's career. To help fill in these remaining information gaps and promote greater transparency regarding selection decisions, we suggest that the Office of the Secretary of Defense (OSD) ask each service to provide detailed specifics on its selection system to researchers and the public. This includes what tests and other factors are used and their respective place and weight in selection for officer commissioning programs, branch, specialty, or job assignment, commissioning, and promotion. To this end, we provide a list of remaining questions and information gaps in Appendix B.

To the best of our knowledge, although this report falls far short of providing a complete picture of the selection systems used by the services, we did not encounter any other source that brings together all the pieces of information shown in this report to afford even a basic view of the different paths through which all the services commission officers and assign them to different career fields. Such a resource could be valuable in helping a potential recruit or candidate to better understand the selection process—in particular, what would make him or her a competitive candidate—and assure him or her that the process is fair. However, until the services make more information available, such a resource cannot be compiled for use.

We do recognize that some information about the selection process might be sensitive and that the services might not want to openly publish everything. Nevertheless, allowing as much transparency as possible would help to better communicate to potential recruits and candidates how the process works. Our study found a shortage of clear and publicly available information on how the selection process works across the services. Furthermore, there appears to be strong demand for such information: In our research, we came across many websites and blogs in which potential recruits and candidates queried how the process works and complained about the lack of official sources or empirically based research to answer their questions.

Standardized Tests Used by the Armed Forces

Because the original intent of this study was to examine the impact that the use of standardized tests in selection decisions could have on racial/ethnic representation in the officer corps and key career fields, this appendix provides a brief review of prior research on the predictive validity and racial/ethnic group differences in mean test scores for the 19 standardized tests identified in our research.[1]

ACT

The ACT is a standardized test that is used to assess ability in English, mathematics, reading, and science.[2] The exam is primarily a multiple-choice test taken over a period of approximately 2 hours and 55 minutes and is administered six times per year. The ACT assessment (with the SAT exam as the alternative) is used for selection into various officer commissioning programs.

Predictive Validity

Given that ACT scores are used predominantly in selection decisions for college admission, the majority of research examining the predictive validity of ACT scores has focused on the academic context. Overall, research finds the ACT is a valid predictor of future performance, including showing a strong positive relationship between ACT scores and first-year student GPA, as well as cumulative college GPA over time.[3]

Racial/Ethnic Group Differences

Like other aptitude tests, the ACT tends to show demographic group differences in mean scores. For example, Camara and Schmidt report average demographic group differences in mean scores for the ACT English, mathematics, reading, and science reasoning exams, as well as the ACT composite score, finding that white students outperform other racial/ethnic groups on all exams except the ACT mathematics test, in which Asian Americans have higher scores.[4] Asian Americans outperform other racial/ethnic groups on the overall ACT composite score. Hispanic students perform slightly better than blacks on all exams, as well as on the ACT com-

---

[1] Although they are separate tests, we count all standardized tests given in TBS for marines as a single test in the number reported here. TBS tests are not included in this appendix, however, because we do not have further information on them.

[2] ACT, 2007.

[3] For a review of recent research, see ACT, 2007.

[4] Camara and Schmidt, 1999.

posite. Research by Noble also finds that the ACT is not biased against racial/ethnic minorities. Specifically, it does not *underpredict* performance (measured by first-year college GPA) of racial/ethnic minorities.[5]

Air Force Officer Qualifying Test

The AFOQT is a multiple-choice test that consists of 11 subtests that are used to create five composite scores: verbal, quantitative, academic aptitude, pilot, and navigator. Five of the 11 AFOQT subtests are used to compute the pilot composite used in the operational selection of Air Force pilot candidates; six are used in the navigator composite. Scores are reported as percentile scores. The Air Force uses the AFOQT to select candidates into AFROTC and OTS programs. The AFOQT is also used to select AFROTC and OTS candidates into aviation career fields; academy graduates are not required to take the AFOQT to apply for pilot training, however.[6]

Predictive Validity

A recent report by Hardison, Sims, and Wong extensively reviews evidence regarding the validity of the AFOQT as a selection tool. Overall, they concluded that there was strong support for the predictive validity of the AFOQT in training situations for officers.[7] For example, work by Arth examined the records of 9,029 nonrated officers who participated in career field training between 1979 and 1983 and found that AFOQT scores had predictive validity for final course grades in almost all of the career field training programs, with most correlations ranging from 0.3 to 0.5.[8] Similarly, a meta-analysis of research on the predictive validity of the AFOQT, by Hartke and Short, found that the academic composite of the AFOQT had a predictive validity of about 0.39 for training grades.[9]

Racial/Ethnic Group Differences

In their review of the AFOQT, Hardison, Sims, and Wong found evidence for significant mean differences in AFOQT scores of officer candidate applicants by racial/ethnic group.[10] For example, a recent examination of the current form of the AFOQT found that, among applicants, mean percentile scores for black, Hispanic, and Asian candidates on each of five composites were lower than for white candidates, with differences in standard deviations ranging from more than one standard deviation on four of the five composites for black candidates to less than half of a standard deviation on all of the composites for Asian candidates.[11] Similarly, Roberts and Skinner found that black OTS participants scored 0.5 standard deviations lower

---

[5]   Noble, 2003.

[6]   Hardison, Sims, and Wong, 2010.

[7]   Hardison, Sims, and Wong, 2010.

[8]   Rated line officers are pilots, combat system officers (navigators), and air battle managers; all other specialties are nonrated. See Arth, 1986.

[9]   Hartke and Short, 1988.

[10]   Hardison, Sims, and Wong, 2010

[11]   Easi.Consult, Schwartz, and Weismuller, 2008.

than white participants did on the verbal, quantitative, and academic ability composites.[12] Carretta and Ree also found that, among Air Force applicants and Air Force pilot trainees, black and Hispanic applicants and trainees performed lower on the AFOQT than white applicants and trainees did.[13]

In their review of the AFOQT, Hardison, Sims, and Wong did not find evidence of predictive bias against racial/ethnic minorities, however.[14] For example, Roberts and Skinner found that, among black OTS participants, AFOQT scores on the academic, verbal, and quantitative composites actually *overpredicted* OTS course grades.[15] The AFOQT quantitative composite also *overpredicted* training performance reviews for black cadets. Similarly, Carretta found that the AFOQT was not biased against blacks or Hispanics in terms of predicting training pass/fail scores for pilots.[16] Finally, Mathews also found that AFOQT scores *overpredicted* performance for black OTS participants.[17]

Alternate Flight Aptitude Selection Test

The AFAST contains seven subtests with a total of 200 questions.[18] The subtests are (1) Background Information, (2) Instrument Comprehension Test, (3) Complex Movements Test, (4) Helicopter Knowledge Test, (5) Cyclic Orientation Test, (6) Mechanical Functions Test, and (7) the Self-Description Form. The AFAST is used during selection for Army Helicopter Flight Training. Specifically, a participant in Army ROTC, OCS, or USMA must take the AFAST to qualify for an aviation branch assignment, with a heavy weight assigned to the AFAST in selection decisions. An applicant for aviation training can retake the exam if he or she fails to perform well on the first try. However, retaking the exam requires authorization from the applicant's commanding officer, and it is permitted only after six months have passed since the first attempt.

Predictive Validity
We found some published research examining the predictive validity of the AFAST. Specifically, a study by Cross looked at performance on the Revised Flight Aptitude Selection Test, the predecessor to the AFAST, as well as the AFAST, and how they related to performance in pilot training.[19] Cross describes the Flight Aptitude Selection Test as having declining predictive validity: Predictive validity for passing flight training declined from 0.31 in 1988 to 0.17 in 1993. However, in the data examined, for every racial and gender group, increasing the cutoff from 90 to 100 or up to 120 would eliminate a disproportionate number of the pilot candidates who failed to pass training. Given the problems with low predictive validity, the Army has

---

[12] Roberts and Skinner, 1996.

[13] Carretta and Ree, 1995.

[14] Hardison, Sims, and Wong, 2010.

[15] Roberts and Skinner, 1996.

[16] Carretta, 1997.

[17] Mathews, 1977.

[18] Headquarters, Department of the Army, 1987.

[19] Cross, 1997.

been in the process of developing a new aviation selection instrument to replace the AFAST. This new test battery, Selection Instrument for Flight Training, is designed to assess cognitive ability, perceptual speed and accuracy, personality and temperament, motivation and attitude, and task prioritization.[20]

Racial/Ethnic Group Differences

At the time of this writing, we are not aware of any published studies examining racial/ethnic group differences in AFAST scores.

Armed Services Vocational Aptitude Battery

The ASVAB is an aptitude test that is required by all of the armed forces to determine eligibility for enlistment.[21] The ASVAB currently contains ten subsections, such as word knowledge, assembling objects, and automotive information. The AFQT score is derived from four of the ASVAB test sections: paragraph comprehension, word knowledge, mathematics knowledge, and arithmetic reasoning.[22]

Certain subtests of the ASVAB are used for selection into some officer commissioning programs. For example, in the Army, an enlisted member applying for a ROTC scholarship must also meet a minimum GT score on the ASVAB—a combination of the verbal expression composite and the arithmetic reasoning subsection. The Army also requires every OCS candidate to take the ASVAB and receive a minimum GT score.[23]

Predictive Validity

There is strong evidence that the AFQT and other composite scores of the ASVAB have predictive validity for a wide variety of outcome measures within the enlisted population. For example, in an extensive review of the literature, Welsh, Kucinkas, and Curran found that AFQT and other ASVAB composite scores had predictive validity for "final school grades, self-paced technical school completion times, first-term attrition, and job performance measures" for enlisted groups.[24] Similarly, research by Orvis, Childress, and Polich found that scores on the AFQT were a significant predictor of performance in simulated missile battle scenarios for enlisted Army personnel and students in training.[25] In another study, Winkler, Fernandez, and Polich found that AFQT scores were significantly related to individual performance and that average AFQT scores for a group were significantly related to group performance for signal operators involved in setting up communication systems for the Army.[26] Whitmarsh and Sulzen also found that GT scores, which are used by the Army in OCS selection, were positively correlated with performance during simulated infantry combat in an enlisted popu-

---

[20] Bruskiewicz et al., 2007.

[21] DoD Instruction (DODI) 1145.01, 2005.

[22] See Pommerich, Segall, and Moreno, 2009.

[23] AR 350-51, 2001.

[24] Welsh, Kucinkas, and Curran, 1990.

[25] Orvis, Childress, and Polich, 1992.

[26] Winkler, Fernandez, and Polich, 1992.

lation.[27] More recently and broadly, Ree and Earles found that, for a wide variety of Air Force enlisted jobs, ASVAB scores were predictive of grades in training schools.[28]

We are aware of only one study that has examined the predictive validity of the ASVAB using an officer population. Read and Whitaker found that marines in OCS who entered under ASVAB waivers because their scores on the electronics composite score did not reach the minimum required were less likely to be successful than their peers who did not require waivers.[29]

Racial/Ethnic Group Differences

Most of the published research on demographic group differences is for enlisted or civilian populations and therefore might not be relevant for officer populations, which are quite different in terms of educational background, as well as demographics, such as race, gender, and age. However, what the available data from youth and enlisted populations show is that mean scores are lower for black and Hispanic groups than for white groups. According to a recent study by Asch and colleagues, roughly 80 percent of white youth would score above the 30th percentile of the AFQT, while only 49 percent of black youth and 53 percent of Hispanic youth would score above the 30th percentile of the AFQT.[30]

There is also some evidence of mean demographic group differences, specifically in officer groups. For example, Read and Whitaker found that black entrants to U.S. Marine Corps OCS were more likely to enter under a waiver for the electronics ASVAB score, meaning that they did not meet minimum score requirements: From fiscal year (FY) 1988 to FY 1992, 29 percent of black OCS entrants required waivers, versus 17 percent of Hispanics and 7 percent of whites.[31] However, the evidence of mean score differences does not suggest that the ASVAB is biased. Like the SAT exam, it does not underpredict the performance of racial and ethnic minorities.[32]

Aviation Selection Test Battery

The ASTB is composed of six subtests focused on the areas of mathematics, reading, mechanical comprehension, spatial apperception, and aviation and nautical information, as well as a supplemental section on aviation.[33] The test can be taken in electronic or paper format and up to three times (with 30 days between the first and second attempts and 90 days between the second and third attempts). Applicants receive combined scores in four areas: an AQR, a PFAR, a FOFAR, and an OAR. The OAR composite score is used as part of the selection process for Navy and Marine Corps OCS. The ASTB is also used in the Navy, Marine Corps, and Coast Guard to select candidates for aviation officer training. The PFAR and FOFAR

---

[27] Whitmarsh and Sulzen, 1989.

[28] Ree and Earles, 1991.

[29] Read and Whitaker, 1993.

[30] Asch, Buck, et al., 2009.

[31] Read and Whitaker, 1993.

[32] Wise et al., 1992.

[33] OPNAV Instruction 1532.1/MCO Instruction 1532.1, 2008.

are used to predict performance during primary flight training for student naval aviators and flight officers, while the AQR and OAR are used to predict academic performance in preflight instruction and ground school.

Predictive Validity

We were able to find some published evidence regarding the predictive validity of the ASTB. In particular, two studies examining the ASTB provide evidence for its predictive validity in terms of training outcomes.[34] First, Brian J. Dean examined how previous batches of pilot trainees would have performed under a certain set of higher ASTB standards for admission. The officers who met the higher standards (and, therefore, who would have been admitted under them) performed one standard deviation better in pilot training at the Naval Aviation Schools Command and had significantly lower attrition rates than the ones who would have not have been selected under the higher standards. Similarly, Helm and Reid found that the ASTB had predictive validity in terms of flight training outcomes for both nonminority and minority candidates, although it *underpredicted* women's performance. Finally, Koch found that receiving a waiver for the ASTB (meaning that the cutoff score was not met) was positively associated with Marine pilot training attrition.[35]

Racial/Ethnic Group Differences

Two studies show that mean ASTB scores are lower for racial/ethnic minority candidates who are accepted to flight training than for white candidates. First, Helm and Reid examined individuals who had completed Aviation Pre-Flight Indoctrination (API), which is a prerequisite for all naval aviator and Naval Flight Officer (NFO) candidates, finding that racial/ethnic minority candidates had lower mean scores on both the AQR and PFAR subscores and lower training scores.[36]

Brian J. Dean found that raising the cutoff for ASTB scores in the Marine Corps would have disproportionately disqualified blacks, Hispanics, and Asians.[37] Specifically, ASTB scores for blacks, Hispanics, and Asians who were selected into aviation training between 1988 and 1992 were lower than for their white peers. Although, overall, the increased cutoff would have disqualified about 39 percent of the group, for each of the minority groups, more than half of the actually selected pilots would not have been selected under the higher standards. Although this finding does not directly give information about ASTB scores in the overall population, or even in the population of applicants, it does suggest that ASTB scores are lower for racial/ethnic minority groups than for nonminority groups.

College-Level Examination Program

Candidates for some postcollege commissioning programs who do not have bachelor's degrees can submit college subject-area test results toward the number of required semester-hours.

---

[34] B. Dean, 1996; Helm and Reid, 2003.

[35] Koch, 2009.

[36] Helm and Reid, 2003.

[37] B. Dean, 1996.

There are several different types of exams that can be used for this purpose. However, these scores are not directly submitted to the services: For instance, for the Army OCS program, these tests must be listed on a college transcript as having entitled the student to credits at that school.[38] Both the Marine Corps and the Navy mention these tests in the context of enlisted-to-officer programs and describe similar requirements: In order to count toward the marine's or seaman's college degree, the college that the applicant attended must have given him or her credit for these tests.[39]

The CLEP is a civilian-developed test that is increasingly given for free to military personnel at various bases and that many colleges accept for class placement or college credit.[40] The passing score for all CLEP subject tests is 50.[41] Passing rates for military examinees in 2007 ranged from 17 percent for college algebra to 64 percent for analyzing and interpreting literature.[42] The tests are 90 minutes long, can be given either on paper or by computer, and can be retaken after six months.[43]

Predictive Validity

We were not able to find any research on the predictive validity of the CLEP in terms of job or training performance outcomes. However, there has been some research focused on comparing CLEP students' knowledge of college material with that of students who take the corresponding class, or otherwise validating allowing students to get course credit via CLEP. For instance, Checketts and Christensen found that students who passed CLEP's general examination in English composition at Utah State University performed comparably on a writing test to students who got As and Bs in the university's freshman English course. In another study, Beanblossom administered CLEP general examinations to 333 University of Washington juniors and found that scores were highly correlated with students' scores on a test they had taken in high school, the Washington Pre-College Test. The author concluded that these tests were not measuring anything distinct from what was measured in these precollege tests. These studies might be of limited utility, however.[44] First, these studies examine students from only one school. Second, the studies tend to be very old, and curricula and tests might have changed since then. Finally, these studies do not examine whether the CLEP has predictive validity in terms of job performance, which would be the most relevant measure in this context.

Racial/Ethnic Group Differences

At the time of this writing, we are not aware of any published studies examining racial/ethnic group differences on the CLEP.

---

[38] Fort Bragg, undated.

[39] OPNAV Instruction 1420.1B, 2009; MCO 1040.43A, 2000.

[40] Defense Activity for Non-Traditional Education Support, undated (c).

[41] U.S. Army Garrison Benelux, 2007.

[42] Defense Activity for Non-Traditional Education Support, undated (b).

[43] Defense Activity for Non-Traditional Education Support, undated (c).

[44] Checketts and Christensen, 1974; Beanblossom, 1969.

English Comprehension Level Test and American Language Course Placement Test

The ECLT and the ALCPT are tests of English proficiency for nonnative English speakers. The ALCPT handbook refers to the ALCPT as a screening test for whether an applicant is proficient enough to take the ECLT but also notes that the tests are statistically equivalent, with an almost-perfect correlation between scores on the two tests.[45] In some military documents, such as AR 350-51, they are referred to interchangeably, suggesting that military candidates whose first language is not English must pass only one of the tests.

The ECLT is a test of listening and reading comprehension of informal U.S. English. Testing can be done either in a 75-minute paper or a substantially shorter computer adaptive version, which can distinguish more finely among high levels of performance.[46] The ALCPT is also both a listening and a reading test. There are 35 different test forms for the ALCPT, each with 66 listening-based questions and 34 written questions.[47]

Military regulations are unclear about how a candidate for an officer commissioning program would be selected to take either of these tests. For instance, the document governing Army OCS (AR 350-51) says that the candidate must take the ECLT "if the applicant's primary language is other than English," which would presumably be noticed by the Army recruiter working with the applicant. However, it is unclear whether this test is given to most U.S. citizens whose primary language is not English: The Air Force's AFRS Instruction 36-2001 says that the "ECLT and [ACLPT] are available only at the MEPS [Military Entrance Processing Station] in San Juan, Puerto Rico."[48] Because being a U.S. citizen and attaining certain scores on the aptitude tests, which assume English-language fluency, are prerequisites for officer selection, we do not see this test as being a major limiting factor in the resulting diversity of the officer corps. A recent study on how requirements for Army OCS affect the eligibility of enlisted soldiers offered this conclusion: "modification of ECLT . . . requirements would produce relatively small increases in the pool of qualified OCS applicants."[49]

The only listed ECLT cutoff score is 80, for Army OCS applicants.[50] This is also listed as a USCGA requirement for international applicants from countries where English is not the primary language.[51] It seems likely that 80 is the ECLT cutoff whenever it is used. We do not know whether the ALCPT has an associated cutoff score.

Predictive Validity

There appears to be limited research on the predictive validity of the ECLT or ALCPT. However, we did identify a study by Robin Dean, Hoffman, and Hoffman for officers and enlisted personnel that found that English proficiency scores on the ECLT and another English language test were "not significantly related to available indicators of success in the Army, [includ-

---

[45] Defense Language Institute English Language Center, 2008a.

[46] Defense Language Institute English Language Center, undated.

[47] Defense Language Institute English Language Center, 2008a.

[48] AFRS Instruction 36-2001, 2008.

[49] M. Smith and Hagman, 2002.

[50] M. Smith and Hagman, 2002.

[51] USCGA, undated (c). International applicants to service academies do not commission into the U.S. military.

ing] rank, level of education, GT and Skills [sic] Qualification Test scores."[52] The researchers concluded that these tests did not include the types of English language skills that were relevant to military service, such as conversational speech and military language.[53]

Racial/Ethnic Group Differences

At the time of this writing, we are not aware of any published studies examining racial/ethnic group differences in ECLT or ALCPT scores.

Law School Admission Test

Law schools use the LSAT to determine admission eligibility. The test consists of five sections, each 35 minutes in length, to measure reading comprehension, analytical reasoning, and logical reasoning. The LSAT is administered four times per year at approved sites.[54]

Predictive Validity

There has been a considerable amount of research on the predictive validity of the LSAT. For example, Schrader provides a very thorough meta-analysis of law school validity studies, with considerable evidence of the predictive validity of the LSAT on first-year law school student GPA performance.[55] Similarly, Linn and Hastings examined the student outcomes for 259,640 students at 154 law schools and found that LSAT predictive validity ranged from 0.14 to 0.66 and had a median value of 0.38. These more recent results report higher validity in predicting first-year law school GPA than Schrader reported and a higher validity than the GPA at the undergraduate institution.[56] We are not aware of any studies examining the predictive validity of the LSAT in a military context, however.

Racial/Ethnic Group Differences

Camara and Schmidt find that, as has been found for other education entrance examinations, white students score highest on the LSAT, with Asians, blacks, and Hispanic students following (based on a sample of LSAT scores for all students applying to law school in 1997–1998).[57] Consistent with these trends is research that is more recent by Diamond-Dalessandro, Suto, and Reese, looking at testing years 2001–2002 to 2007–2008 and finding that LSAT scores have been consistently lower for black and Hispanic law school applicants than for white and Asian law school applicants. Mean scores were 142 for blacks, between 146 and 147 for Hispanics, 152 for Asians, and between 152 and 153 for whites in each of these testing years.[58]

---

[52] The Skill Qualification Tests are no longer in use.

[53] R. Dean, Hoffman, and Hoffman, 1988.

[54] Law School Admissions Council, undated.

[55] Schrader, 1977.

[56] Linn and Hastings, 1984.

[57] Camara and Schmidt, 1999.

[58] The LSAT has separate categories for Hispanic, Puerto Rican, and Mexican American applicants, which appear to be exclusive categories that are based on self-identification (Diamond-Dalessandro, Suto, and Reese, 2008).

Physical Fitness Assessment

Each branch of the military has a main physical fitness test that is given regularly to all personnel except those who cannot take it because of injury, pregnancy, or deployment. Each test is made up of subtests, which are scored independently; scoring varies based on age and sex. Other physical fitness tests are also given to certain populations, such as for admission into service academies and selection into special forces. Each service's test and scoring are distinct from those of other services. The primary tests are the APFT, the Air Force PFT, CFA, the Marine Corps PFT, the Navy PRT, and the Coast Guard PFE. Applicants for four-year scholarships to the Army ROTC program must also pass the President's Challenge PFT. The Marine Corps is in the midst of adopting an additional test for all marines called the Combat Fitness Test (CFT). Unlike the standard Marine Corps PFT, this was not listed as a requirement for recent Marine Corps OCS boards.[59] Finally, there are specialized physical fitness screening tests required for any Naval academy midshipmen who wish to join the Navy SEALs or obtain EOD rating.

Predictive Validity

At the time of this writing, we are not aware of any published studies examining the predictive validity of the physical fitness tests on key officer outcomes in the selection contexts on which this research focuses.

Racial/Ethnic Group Differences

Although we did not find publicly available data on physical fitness scores by race/ethnicity for officer candidates, some things can be inferred from the wider literature. First, there is no body of literature suggesting practically important overall differences in physical fitness across racial/ethnic groups on par with aptitude-score differences. The major demographic group difference in terms of physical abilities that is relevant to the military is the difference between men and women, for which military physical fitness tests adjust in terms of subtest scoring and, to a much lesser extent, subtest events.

Of those studies that have examined potential differences, those comparing physical fitness test scores across racial/ethnic groups within the military context show varied results. For example, Robbins and colleagues, examining a population of both enlisted and officers, found that being black was negatively associated with physical fitness as measured by passing the Air Force PFT. Officers and enlisted were modeled together, and officers had a lower risk of failure.[60] Bell and colleagues examined Army Basic Combat trainees and found that black trainees initially performed significantly better on their APFTs than white trainees, both for male and female groups.[61] Army Basic Combat Training is primarily, but not exclusively, enlisted, however. Finally, Knapik and colleagues found minimal racial/ethnic group differences among recruits entering Army Basic Training.[62] Thus, overall, these studies suggest that any differences among racial groups in terms of physical fitness scores are likely minimal. Addi-

---

[59]   Marine Administrative Message (MARADMIN) 383/10, 2010.

[60]   Robbins et al., 2001.

[61]   Bell et al., 1994.

[62]   Knapik et al., 2004.

tionally, physical fitness test scores are unique among standardized test scores in terms of how responsive they are to physical training. For instance, Christianson found that, in a group of AFROTC participants, Air Force PFT scores and pass rates were quite responsive to various types of regular physical fitness training.[63]

SAT Exam

The SAT Reasoning Test is a private sector–developed standardized test that colleges use to evaluate applicants and is typically taken during the junior or senior year of high school.[64] The exam lasts three hours and 45 minutes and covers three primary sections: reading, mathematics, and writing. It is offered seven times during the calendar year in the United States.[65] Scores for the three sections derive from equally weighted questions that are worth one point for a correct answer and −0.25 point for each marked incorrectly.[66] Students can retake the test.[67] Like the ACT, the SAT exam is used for selection into various officer commissioning programs.

Predictive Validity

A considerable amount of research has been conducted examining the predictive validity of the SAT exam. Overall, SAT exam scores are consistently found to be a significant predictor of first-year college GPA and have been found to predict academic achievement throughout the college years.[68]

Racial/Ethnic Group Differences

Like the ACT, the SAT exam shows racial/ethnic differences in mean scores. For example, Camara and Schmidt report that blacks and Hispanics score considerably lower on average than whites, while Asians score slightly lower than whites on the verbal subtest (one-quarter standard deviation) but have very similar mean scores on the quantitative subtest.[69] The data from the College Board regarding 2010 college-bound seniors show somewhat similar results. Mean critical reading and math scores were 429 and 428, respectively, for blacks; 519 and 591 for Asians, Asian Americans, and Pacific Islanders; and 528 and 536 for whites. Hispanics were separated into several different categories (e.g., Mexican, Puerto Rican, South American) with mean critical reading scores of 454 and mean math scores ranging from 452 to 467.[70] Despite these subgroup differences, research shows that the SAT exam is not biased against

---

[63] Christianson, 2009.

[64] SAT Reasoning Test is a registered trademark of the College Board.

[65] College Board, undated (a).

[66] College Board, undated (c).

[67] College Board, undated (d).

[68] Boldt, 1986; Kobrin et al., 2008; Wilson, 1983.

[69] Camara and Schmidt, 1999

[70] College Board, 2010.

racial/ethnic minorities, meaning that it does not *underpredict* the performance of racial/ethnic minorities.[71]

Test of Basic Aviation Skills

The TBAS measures cognitive, multitasking, and psychomotor attributes.[72] Taken over the course of an hour, the TBAS is a computer-based test that incorporates keypads, joystick movement, and foot pedal response as test indicators. The TBAS includes the following subtests: (1) directional orientation test, (2) three-digit and five-digit listening test, (3) horizontal tracking test, (4) airplane tracking test, (5) airplane and horizontal tracking, and (6) an emergency scenario test. The TBAS is used to aid in the selection of Air Force pilot candidates from AFROTC and OTS. The TBAS score is combined with the AFOQT pilot composite score and the number of flying hours to compose the PCSM score that is reviewed by the pilot selection board.

Predictive Validity

In an Air Force–sponsored study, Carretta found that TBAS subscores have predictive validity in terms of training outcomes. Carretta examined the records of 994 Air Force officers who attended Specialized Undergraduate Pilot Training. He found that several of the TBAS subtests had predictive validity in terms of performance in pilot training, both for likelihood of attrition from the training program and for final grades.[73]

Racial/Ethnic Group Differences

At the time of this writing, we are not aware of any published studies examining racial/ethnic group differences in TBAS scores.

---

[71] Mattern et al., 2008.

[72] PCSM, undated (c).

[73] Carretta, 2005.

Questions for the Services

As discussed in Chapter Four, there are remaining information gaps and questions that need to be filled in order to have a complete picture of the selection systems being used by the services and the role of standardized tests within the broader selection system. This appendix provides a list of those key questions regarding current data gaps for each service and respective officer commissioning program.

Army

Reserve Officers' Training Corps
Selection into the Program. This section lists outstanding questions regarding selection into Army ROTC.

- Are the requirements for selection and weights of each factor correctly outlined in this document?
- For all *scholarship* applicants:
  – Can any requirements be waived or substituted? Under what conditions? By whom and what is allowed for substitution?
- For *active-duty enlisted scholarship* applicants to the Green to Gold program:
  – What are the weights given to each factor that composes the whole-person score?
  – Can any requirements be waived or substituted? Under what conditions? By whom and what is allowed for substitution?
- For all *nonscholarship* applicants:
  – What are the requirements for admission other than the APFT?
  – What are the weights for these requirements in selection decisions?
  – Can any requirements be waived or substituted? Under what conditions? By whom and what is allowed for substitution?

Branch, Specialty, or Job Selection. This section lists outstanding questions regarding branch, specialty, or job selection for Army ROTC.

- Are the factors, weights of each factor in the OMS, and overall selection process correctly outlined in this document?
- Are standardized tests required for selection into any other branch besides aviation?
- For aviation candidates, in addition to the AFAST, what other factors are used in the selection decision?

- What are the weights for these factors in selection decisions?
- Can any requirements be waived or substituted? Under what conditions? By whom and what is allowed to be substituted?

Officer Candidate School

Selection into the Program. This section lists outstanding questions regarding selection into Army OCS.

- Are the requirements for selection correctly outlined in this document?
- What other factors go into selection decisions?
- What are the weights for each factor (including standardized test scores) in the selection decision?
- Can any requirements be waived or substituted? Under what conditions? By whom and what is allowed for substitution?
- Do requirements differ for prior or active-duty enlisted applicants?

Branch, Specialty, or Job Selection. This section lists outstanding questions regarding branch, specialty, or job selection for Army OCS.

- Are the requirements for selection correctly outlined in this document?
- Are standardized tests required for selection into any other career field besides aviation?
- How does the assignment process work?
  - What factors are used in the assignment decisions?
  - What are the weights for these factors in selection decisions?

U.S. Military Academy

Selection into the Program. This section lists outstanding questions regarding selection into USMA.

- Are the requirements for selection correctly outlined in this document?
- For each of the three factors used in the whole-person score, what are the individual components included in each factor?
  - What are the individual weights of each component in the total factor score?
- Can any requirements be waived or substituted? Under what conditions? By whom and what is allowed for substitution?
- Do requirements differ for prior or active-duty enlisted applicants?
- When adjustments are made to the final score due to the use of a whole-person approach, does the adjustment mean that the weights can shift across categories (for example, 50 percent academic, 35 percent leadership, and 15 percent physical)? Or are the "shifts" within a category (for example, graduating top of the class can replace SAT exam or ACT scores)?

Branch, Specialty, or Job Selection. This section lists outstanding questions regarding branch, specialty, or job selection in USMA.

- Are the factors, weights of each factor, and overall selection process correctly outlined in this document?
- Are standardized tests required for selection into any other branch besides aviation?
- For aviation candidates, in addition to the AFAST, what other factors are used in the selection decision?
  - What are the weights for these factors in selection decisions?
  - Can any requirements be waived or substituted? Under what conditions? By whom and what is allowed for substitution?

Air Force

Reserve Officer Training Corps

Selection into the Program. This section lists outstanding questions regarding selection into AFROTC.

- Are the current requirements for selection and weights of each factor correctly outlined in this document?
- Under what circumstances can the minimum AFOQT scores be waived?
  - Who grants the waiver, and how often are these waivers given?
- For all *scholarship* applicants:
  - What are the weights for each factor in selection decisions?
  - Can any requirements be waived or substituted? Under what conditions? By whom and what is allowed for substitution?

Branch, Specialty, or Job Selection. This section lists outstanding questions regarding branch, specialty, or job selection in AFROTC.

- Are there two separate processes for selection of Air Force specialties: one for rated line officers (pilots [including pilots of remotely piloted aircraft], combat system officers, and air battle managers) and one for nonrated line officers?
- For each board process, what factors are used to create the OML ranking cadets?
  - What are the weights for these factors?
- How does the assignment process work using the OML, cadet preferences, and manpower requirements?
- Are standardized tests required for selection into any other branch besides aviation?
- For aviation candidates, is there a minimum PCSM score that must be achieved?
  - How are the AFOQT and TBAS weighted in determining the PCSM score?

Officer Training School

Selection into the Program. This section lists outstanding questions regarding selection into Air Force OTS.

- Are the requirements for selection correctly outlined in this document?
- Can any requirements be waived or substituted? Under what conditions? By whom and what is allowed for substitution?

- Do requirements differ for prior or active-duty enlisted applicants?

Branch, Specialty, or Job Selection. This section lists outstanding questions regarding branch, specialty, or job selection in Air Force OTS.

- Are the requirements for selection correctly outlined in this document?
- Are standardized tests required for selection into any other career field besides aviation?
- How does the assignment process work?
  - What factors are used in the assignment decisions?
  - What are the weights for these factors in selection decisions?

U.S. Air Force Academy

Selection into the Program. This section lists outstanding questions regarding selection into USAFA.

- Are the requirements for selection correctly outlined in this document?
- For each of the three factors used in the whole-person score, what are the individual components included in the factor?
  - What are the individual weights of each component in the total factor score?
- Can any requirements be waived or substituted? Under what conditions? By whom and what is allowed for substitution?
- Do requirements differ for prior or active-duty enlisted applicants?
- When adjustments are made to the final score due to the use of a whole-person approach, does the adjustment mean that the weights can shift across categories (for example, 50 percent academic, 35 percent leadership, and 15 percent physical)? Or are the "shifts" within a category (for example, graduating top of the class can replace SAT exam or ACT scores)?

Branch, Specialty, or Job Selection. This section lists outstanding questions regarding branch, specialty, or job selection in USAFA.

- Are the requirements and assignment process correctly outlined in this document?
- What information is provided to the board when they rank cadets?
- What weight is each of the three factors given in determining the order of merit?
- How does the assignment process work?
  - What factors are used in the assignment decisions?
  - What are the weights for these factors in selection decisions?
  - Who are the Air Force officers who sit on the two panels?
  - Do the two panels work simultaneously and rate the same way on the same factors with the same weights and scores or ratings?
  - How are the two merit lists reconciled to make final selection decisions?
- Are any standardized tests required for assignment to particular career fields?

Navy

Reserve Officers Training Corps

Selection into the Program. This section lists outstanding questions regarding selection into NROTC.

- Are the requirements for selection correctly outlined in this document?
- For all *scholarship* applicants:
  - What are all the factors that are used to select applicants for scholarships?
  - What are the weights for these factors (including standardized test scores) in selection decisions?
  - Can any requirements be waived or substituted? Under what conditions? By whom and what is allowed for substitution?
  - Do requirements differ for prior or active-duty enlisted applicants?
- For all *nonscholarship* applicants:
  - What are the requirements for admission?
  - What are the weights for these requirements in selection decisions?
  - Can any requirements be waived or substituted? Under what conditions? By whom and what is allowed for substitution?
  - Do requirements differ for prior or active-duty enlisted applicants?

Branch, Specialty, or Job Selection. This section lists outstanding questions regarding branch, specialty, or job selection in NROTC.

- Are OMSs calculated separately for those seeking aviation and nonaviation jobs?
- Are the factors and weights for each factor in the selection process correctly outlined in this document?
- How is aptitude measured?
- Can these requirements be waived or substituted? Under what conditions? By whom and with what alternative?
- Are there other factors in compiling OMSs and rankings?
- What weights are given to candidate preference, rank order, and Navy manpower requirements during the assignment process?
- Are standardized tests required for selection into any other branch besides aviation?

Officer Candidate School

Selection into the Program. This section lists outstanding questions regarding selection into Navy OCS.

- Are the requirements for selection correctly outlined in this document?
- What other factors go into selection decisions?
- What are the weights for each factor (including standardized test scores) in the selection decision?
- Can any requirements be waived or substituted? Under what conditions? By whom and what is allowed for substitution?
- Do requirements differ for prior or active-duty enlisted applicants?

Branch, Specialty, or Job Selection. This section lists outstanding questions regarding branch, specialty, or Job selection in Navy OCS.

- Are the requirements for selection correctly outlined in this document?
- Are standardized tests required for selection into any other career field besides aviation?
- How does the assignment process work?
  - What factors are used in the assignment decisions?
  - What are the weights for these factors in selection decisions?

U.S. Naval Academy

Selection into the Program. This section lists outstanding questions regarding selection into USNA.

- Are the requirements for selection correctly outlined in this document?
- For each of the three factors used in the whole-person score, what are the individual components included in each factor?
  - What are the individual weights of each component in the total factor score?
- Can any requirements be waived or substituted? Under what conditions? By whom and what is allowed for substitution?
- Do requirements differ for prior or active-duty enlisted applicants?
- When adjustments are made to the final score due to the use of a whole-person approach, does the adjustment mean that the weights can shift across categories (for example, 50 percent academic, 35 percent leadership, and 15 percent physical)? Or are the "shifts" within a category (for example, graduating top of the class can replace SAT exam or ACT scores)?

Branch, Specialty, or Job Selection. This section lists outstanding questions regarding branch, specialty, or job selection in USNA.

- Are the requirements and assignment process correctly outlined in this document?
- Are standardized tests required for selection into any other career field besides aviation, the SEALs, and EOD?
- How does the assignment process work?
  - What factors are used in the assignment decisions?
  - What are the weights for these factors in selection decisions?

Marine Corps

Reserve Officers' Training Corps

Selection into the Program. This section lists outstanding questions regarding selection into NROTC (Marine Corps option).

- Are the requirements for selection correctly outlined in this document?
- For all *scholarship* applicants:
  - What are all the factors that are used to select applicants for scholarships?

- What are the weights for these factors (including standardized test scores) in selection decisions?
- Can any requirements be waived or substituted? Under what conditions? By whom and what is allowed for substitution?
- Do requirements differ for prior or active-duty enlisted applicants?
- For all *nonscholarship* applicants:
  - What are the requirements for admission?
  - What are the weights for these requirements in selection decisions?
  - Can any requirements be waived or substituted? Under what conditions? By whom and what is allowed for substitution?
  - Do requirements differ for prior or active-duty enlisted applicants?

Branch, Specialty, or Job Selection. This section lists outstanding questions regarding branch, specialty, or job selection in NROTC (Marine Corps option).

- Are the factors and weights for each factor in the selection process correctly outlined in this document?
- Are standardized tests required for selection into any other branch besides aviation?
- For aviation candidates, in addition to the ASTB, what other factors are used in the selection decision?
  - What are the weights for these factors in selection decisions?
  - Can any requirements be waived or substituted? Under what conditions? By whom and what is allowed for substitution?

Officer Candidate School

Selection into the Program. This section lists outstanding questions regarding selection into Marine Corps OCS.

- Are the requirements for selection correctly outlined in this document?
- What other factors go into selection decisions?
- What are the weights for each factor (including standardized test scores) in the selection decision?
- Can any requirements be waived or substituted? Under what conditions? By whom and what is allowed for substitution?
- Do requirements differ for prior or active-duty enlisted applicants?

Branch, Specialty, or Job Selection. This section lists outstanding questions regarding branch, specialty, or job selection in Marine Corps OCS.

- Are the requirements for selection correctly outlined in this document?
- Are standardized tests required for selection into any other career field besides aviation?
- How does the assignment process work?
  - What factors are used in the assignment decisions?
  - What are the weights for these factors in selection decisions?

U.S. Naval Academy

For oustanding questions regarding Marine Corps candidates at USNA, see the previous sections on USNA and Marine Corps branch, specialty, or job selection.

Coast Guard

Officer Candidate School

Selection into the Program. This section lists outstanding questions regarding selection into Coast Guard OCS.

- Are the requirements for selection correctly outlined in this document?
- What other factors go into selection decisions?
- What are the weights for each factor (including standardized test scores) in the selection decision?
- Can any requirements be waived or substituted? Under what conditions? By whom and what is allowed for substitution?
- Do requirements differ for prior or active-duty enlisted applicants?

Branch, Specialty, or Job Selection. This section lists outstanding questions regarding branch, specialty, or job selection in Coast Guard OCS.

- Are the requirements for selection correctly outlined in this document?
- Are standardized tests required for selection into any other career field besides aviation?
- How does the assignment process work?
  - What factors are used in the assignment decisions?
  - What are the weights for these factors in selection decisions?

U.S. Coast Guard Academy

Selection into the Program. This section lists outstanding questions regarding selection into USCGA.

- Are the requirements for selection correctly outlined in this document?
- What other factors go into selection decisions?
- What are the weights for each factor (including standardized test scores) in the selection decision?
- Can any requirements be waived or substituted? Under what conditions? By whom and what is allowed for substitution?
- Do requirements differ for prior or active-duty enlisted applicants?
- How does the board process work?

Branch, Specialty, or Job Selection. This section lists outstanding questions regarding branch, specialty, or job selection in USCGA.

- Are the requirements for selection correctly outlined in this document?
- Are standardized tests required for selection into any other career field besides aviation?

- How does the assignment process work?
  - What factors are used in the assignment decisions?
  - What are the weights for these factors in selection decisions?

Bibliography

ACT, *Prediction Research Summary Tables*, Iowa City, Ia., 1998.

———, *The ACT Technical Manual*, Iowa City, Ia., 2007. As of August 18, 2011:
http://www.act.org/aap/pdf/ACT_Technical_Manual.pdf

"AFOQT: How to Prepare, How to Succeed," *Baseops.net*, undated. As of August 19, 2011:
http://www.baseops.net/afoqt/

AFROTC—*See* U.S. Air Force Reserve Officer Training Corps.

AFRS Instruction 36-2001—*See* Air Force Recruiting Service, 2008.

Air Force Recruiting Service, *Recruiting Procedures for the Air Force*, Instruction 36-2001, April 1, 2005, incorporating through change 2, September 8, 2008. As of October 8, 2010:
http://www.af.mil/shared/media/epubs/AFRSI36-2001.pdf

Air Force Reserve Officer Training Corps Detachment 485 at Rutgers University, "AFOQT," undated. As of July 7, 2011:
http://afrotc.rutgers.edu/afoqt.html

Air University, "Applying to OTS," undated (a). As of November 9, 2009:
http://www.au.af.mil/au/holmcenter/OTS/BOT/botapply.asp

———, "Greetings from the Commander," undated (b). As of February 17, 2012:
http://www.au.af.mil/au/holmcenter/ots/

———, "Enlisted Commissioning Opportunities," June 4, 2008; referenced January 11, 2010.

Aleamoni, Lawrence M., and Linda Oboler, "ACT Versus SAT in Predicting First Semester GPA," *Educational and Psychological Measurement*, Vol. 38, No. 2, July 1978, pp. 393–399.

Allen, Jeff, and Steven B. Robbins, "Prediction of College Major Persistence Based on Vocational Interests, Academic Preparation, and First-Year Academic Performance," *Higher Education Research*, Vol. 49, No. 1, February 2008, pp. 62–79.

American Educational Research Association, American Psychological Association, and National Council on Measurement in Education Joint Committee on Standards for Educational and Psychological Testing, *Standards for Educational and Psychological Testing*, Washington, D.C.: American Educational Research Association, 1999.

Angoff, William H., and Susan F. Ford, "Item-Race Interaction on a Test of Scholastic Aptitude," *Journal of Educational Measurement*, Vol. 10, No. 2, Summer 1973, pp. 95–106.

AR 350-51—*See* Headquarters, Department of the Army, 2001.

Arabian, Jane M., and Jennifer A. Shelby, *Policies, Procedures, and People: The Initial Selection of U.S. Military Officers*, Washington, D.C.: Office of the Assistant Secretary of Defense for Force Management Policy, Directorate for Accession Policy, November 1999. As of August 18, 2011:
http://www.dtic.mil/dtic/tr/fulltext/u2/p010347.pdf

Armor, David J., and Curtis L. Gilroy, "Changing Minority Representation in the U.S. Military," *Armed Forces and Society*, Vol. 36, No. 2, January 2010, pp. 223–246.

Arnold, Richard D., and Jeffrey B. Phillips, *Causes of Student Attrition in U.S. Naval Aviation Training: A Five Year Review from FY 2003 to FY 2007*, Pensacola, Fla.: Naval Aerospace Medical Research Laboratory, technical memorandum, 2008. As of August 18, 2011:
http://www.dtic.mil/cgi-bin/GetTRDoc?Location=U2&doc=GetTRDoc.pdf&AD=ADA494839

Arth, Thomas O., *Validation of the AFOQT for Non-Rated Officers*, Brooks Air Force Base, Texas: Air Force Human Resources Laboratory, Air Force Systems Command, technical paper 85-50, January 1986.

Asch, Beth J., Christopher Buck, Jacob Alex Klerman, Meredith Kleykamp, and David S. Loughran, *Military Enlistment of Hispanic Youth: Obstacles and Opportunities*, Santa Monica, Calif.: RAND Corporation, MG-773-OSD, 2009. As of August 18, 2011:
http://www.rand.org/pubs/monographs/MG773.html

Asch, Beth J., Paul Heaton, and Bogdan Savych, *Recruiting Minorities: What Explains Recent Trends in the Army and Navy?* Santa Monica, Calif.: RAND Corporation, MG-861-OSD, 2009. As of August 18, 2011:
http://www.rand.org/pubs/monographs/MG861.html

Barrick, Murray R., and Michael K. Mount, "The Big Five Personality Dimensions and Job Performance: A Meta-Analysis," *Personnel Psychology*, Vol. 44, No. 1, March 1991, pp. 1–26.

———, "Yes, Personality Matters: Moving on to More Important Matters," *Human Performance*, Vol. 18, No. 4, 2005, pp. 359–372.

Bartone, P. T., *Personality Hardiness as a Predictor of Officer Cadet Leadership Performance*, West Point, N.Y.: U.S. Military Academy, Department of Behavioral Sciences and Leadership, 2000.

Barucky, Jerry M., and Brice M. Stone, *Difficulties in Accessing a Representative Pilot Force: The Demographic Challenge and Views of Minority Pilot Focus Groups*, San Antonio, Texas: Metrica, 2000.

Bass, Bernard M., and Charles H. Coates, "Forecasting Officer Potential Using the Leaderless Group Discussion," *Journal of Abnormal and Social Psychology*, Vol. 47, No. 2, Supp., April 1952, pp. 321–325.

Beanblossom, Gary F., *What Do the CLEP General Examinations Measure?* Seattle, Wash.: University of Washington, 1969.

Bell, Nicole, Paul Amoroso, David Hemenway, Tom Mangione, and Bruce Jones, *Race and Injury Among Army Basic Trainees*, Natick, Mass.: U.S. Army Research Institute of Environmental Medicine, May 1994. As of August 18, 2011:
http://handle.dtic.mil/100.2/ADA306072

Besetsny, Leasley K., Malcolm James Ree, and James A. Earles, "Special Test for Computer Programmers? Not Needed: The Predictive Efficiency of the Electronic Data Processing Test for a Sample of Air Force Recruits," *Educational and Psychological Measurement*, Vol. 53, No. 2, Summer 1993, pp. 507–511.

Blake, Rex J., Earl H. Potter, and Richard E. Slimak, "Validation of the Structural Scales of the CPI for Predicting the Performance of Junior Officers in the U.S. Coast Guard," *Journal of Business and Psychology*, Vol. 7, No. 4, June 1993, pp. 431–448.

Boldt, Robert F., *Generalization of SAT Validity Across Colleges*, New York: College Entrance Examination Board, report 86-3, 1986.

Bowers, Kendra M., *The Utility of the Myers-Briggs Type Indicator and the Strong Interest Inventory in Predicting Service Community Selection at the United States Naval Academy*, Monterey, Calif.: Naval Postgraduate School, 2002.

Brodnick, R. J., and Malcolm James Ree, "Factorially Equivalent Test Batteries," *Military Psychology*, Vol. 9, No. 3, 1997, pp. 187–198.

Brown, Dianne C., Janice H. Laurence, and Deborah B. Eitelberg, *Demographics and Performance of Military Officers in Relation to Aptitude*, Alexandria, Va.: Human Resources Research Organization, FR-PRD-89-12, June 1989.

Bruskiewicz, Kenneth T., Lawrence C. Katz, Janis Houston, Cheryl Paullin, Gavan O'Shea, and Diane Damos, *Predictor Development and Pilot Testing of a Prototype Selection Instrument for Army Flight Training*, Arlington, Va.: U.S. Army Research Institute for the Behavioral and Social Sciences, technical report 1195, February 2007. As of August 18, 2011:
http://purl.access.gpo.gov/GPO/LPS94179

Burke, Emmett E., *Black Officer Under-Representation in Combat Arms Branches*, Fort Leavenworth, Kan.: School of Advanced Military Studies, U.S. Army Command and General Staff College, AY 01-02, 2002. As of August 18, 2011:
http://handle.dtic.mil/100.2/ADA402652

Camara, Wayne J., and Gary Echternacht, "The SAT I and High School Grades: Utility in Predicting Success in College," *Research Notes*, RN-10, July 2000. As of August 18, 2011:
http://professionals.collegeboard.com/data-reports-research/cb/sat-grades-utility-predicting

Camara, Wayne J., and Amy Elizabeth Schmidt, *Group Differences in Standardized Testing and Social Stratification*, New York: College Entrance Examination Board, report 99-5, 1999.

Carretta, Thomas R., "Group Differences on US Air Force Pilot Selection Tests," *International Journal of Selection and Assessment*, Vol. 5, No. 2, April 1997, pp. 115–127.

———, "U.S. Air Force Pilot Selection and Training Methods," *Aviation, Space, and Environmental Medicine*, Vol. 71, No. 9, September 2000, pp. 950–956.

———, *Development and Validation of the Test of Basic Aviation Skills (TBAS)*, Wright-Patterson Air Force Base, Ohio: Human Effectiveness Directorate, Warfighter Interface Division, AFRL-HE-WP-TR-2005-0172, 2005. As of August 18, 2011:
http://handle.dtic.mil/100.2/ADA442563

Carretta, Thomas R., and Malcolm James Ree, "Air Force Officer Qualifying Test Validity for Predicting Pilot Training Performance," *Journal of Business and Psychology*, Vol. 9, No. 4, June 1995, pp. 379–388.

Carroll, John B., and John L. Horn, "On the Scientific Basis of Ability Testing," *American Psychologist*, Vol. 36, No. 10, October 1981, pp. 1012–1020.

Cascio, Elizabeth U., and Ethan G. Lewis, "Schooling and the Armed Forces Qualifying Test: Evidence from School-Entry Laws," *Journal of Human Resources*, Vol. 41, No. 2, Spring 2006, pp. 294–318.

Checketts, Keith T., and Mark G. Christensen, "The Validity of Awarding Credit by Examination in English Composition," *Educational and Psychological Measurement*, Vol. 34, No. 2, July 1974, pp. 357–361.

Chief of Naval Operations, *Physical Readiness Program*, Chief of Naval Operations Instruction 6110.H, August 15, 2005. As of October 8, 2010:
http://doni.daps.dla.mil/Directives/06000%20Medical%20and%20Dental%20Services/
06-100%20General%20Physical%20Fitness/6110.1H.pdf

———, *Enlisted to Officer Commissioning Programs Application Administrative Manual*, Chief of Naval Operations Instruction 1420.1B, December 14, 2009. As of October 8, 2010:
http://doni.daps.dla.mil/Directives/01000%20Military%20Personnel%20Support/
01-400%20Promotion%20and%20Advancement%20Programs/1420.%201B.pdf

Chief of Naval Operations and Commandant of the Marine Corps, *U.S. Navy and Marine Corps Aviation Selection Test Battery*, Chief of Naval Operations Instruction 1532.1, Marine Corps Order 1532.1, Navy Bureau of Medicine and Surgery Instruction M3B4, March 13, 2008. As of December 10, 2009:
http://www.med.navy.mil/directives/oth/OPNAV%201532.1.pdf

Christianson, Alec, *A Comparison of Regimented, Scheduled, and Individualized Army Physical Fitness Test Training Programs*, Stout, Wis.: University of Wisconsin, master's thesis, 2009. As of August 19, 2011:
http://www.uwstout.edu/lib/thesis/2009/2009christiansona.pdf

Cleary, T. Anne, "Test Bias: Prediction of Grades of Negro and White Students in Integrated Colleges," *Journal of Educational Measurement*, Vol. 5, No. 2, Summer 1968, pp. 115–124.

Cohen, Jacob, "A Power Primer," *Psychological Bulletin*, Vol. 112, No. 1, July 1992, pp. 155–159.

College Board, "About the SAT®," undated (a). As of October 6, 2010:
http://professionals.collegeboard.com/testing/sat-reasoning/about

——, "CLEP," undated (b). As of August 19, 2011:
http://clep.collegeboard.org

——, "How the SAT Is Scored," undated (c); referenced October 6, 2010. As of August 25, 2011:
http://sat.collegeboard.org/scores/how-sat-is-scored

——, "Retaking the SAT," undated (d). As of October 6, 2010:
http://professionals.collegeboard.com/testing/sat-reasoning/scores/retake

——, "SAT® Percentile Ranks, 2010 College-Bound Seniors: Critical Reading, Mathematics and Writing Percentile Ranks by Gender and Ethnic Groups," 2010. As of October 4, 2010:
http://professionals.collegeboard.com/profdownload/sat-percentile-ranks-by-gender-ethnicity-2010.pdf

College Board and National Merit Scholarship Corporation, *Official Student Guide to the PSAT/NMSQT: Preliminary SAT/National Merit Scholarship Qualifying Test*, 76909-01442-UNLWEB79, 2009.

Collins, Judith M., and David H. Gleaves, "Race, Job Applicants, and the Five-Factor Model of Personality: Implications for Black Psychology, Industrial/Organizational Psychology, and the Five-Factor Theory," *Journal of Applied Psychology*, Vol. 83, No. 4, August 1998, pp. 531–544.

Commandant of the Marine Corps, *Enlisted-to-Officer Commissioning Programs*, Marine Corps Order 1040.43A, May 2, 2000. As of October 8, 2010:
http://www.usmc.mil/news/publications/Documents/MCO%201040.43A.pdf

Cook, Gen (ret.) Donald G., "Accession Update," briefing slides, Washington, D.C.: Headquarters, U.S. Air Force, 2004.

Cooper, Matt, "Minority Attrition Study," briefing slides, Headquarters, U.S. Air Force, Air Education and Training Command, 2003.

Cowan, Douglas K., Linda E. Barrett, and Toni Giuliano Wegner, *Air Force Reserve Officer Training Corps Selection System Validation*, Brooks Air Force Base, Texas: Air Force Human Resources Laboratory, Air Force Systems Command, technical report 88-54, December 1989.

Cross, Kenneth, *Current State of Army Aviator Selection*, Charlottesville, Va.: U.S. Army Research Institute for the Behavioral and Social Sciences, AD-a336 143, 1997.

Damos, Diane L., and R. Bruce Gould, *Feasibility of Developing a Common U.S. Army Helicopter Pilot Candidate Selection System: Analysis of U.S. Air Force Data*, Arlington, Va.: U.S. Army Research Institute for the Behavioral and Social Sciences, 2007. As of August 19, 2011:
http://handle.dtic.mil/100.2/ADA475416

De Corte, Wilfried, Filip Lievens, and Paul R. Sackett, "Combining Predictors to Achieve Optimal Trade-Offs Between Selection Quality and Adverse Impact," *Journal of Applied Psychology*, Vol. 92, No. 5, September 2007, pp. 1380–1393.

Dean, Brian J., *Aviation Selection Testing: The Effect of Minimum Scores on Minorities*, Monterey, Calif.: Naval Postgraduate School, master's thesis, March 1996. As of August 19, 2011:
http://handle.dtic.mil/100.2/ADA307314

Dean, Robin A., Lee M. Hoffman, and Diane M. Hoffman, *Evaluation of English Language Needs, Preparation, and Screening Among Non-Native English Speaking Officers and Soldiers*, Washington, D.C.: American Institutes for Research, ADA203611, 1988.

Defense Activity for Non-Traditional Education Support, "2010–2011 Calendar of National Testing Programs," undated (a).

——, "CLEP Subject (Paper-Based) Volume and Pass Rate FY07," undated (b).

——, "College Level Examination Program (CLEP)," undated (c).

——, "DSST," undated (d).

——, "Excelsior College Examinations (ECE)," undated (e).

Defense Language Institute English Language Center, "English Comprehension Level Text," undated; referenced October 4, 2010. As of August 19, 2011:
http://www.dlielc.edu/Testing/ecl_test.html

———, *American Language Course Placement Test Handbook, Department of the Air Force, Officer Promotions and Selective Continuation*, Air Force Instruction 36-2501, July 16, 2004, incorporating change 2, September 13, 2007.

———, *American Language Course Placement Test Handbook*, Lackland Air Force Base, Texas, February 2008a.

———, *Air Force Military Personnel Testing System*, Washington, D.C., Air Force Instruction 36-2605, September 24, 2008b. As of December 1, 2009:
http://www.e-publishing.af.mil/shared/media/epubs/AFI36-2605.pdf

Diamond-Dalessandro, Susan P., Deborah A. Suto, and Lynda M. Reese, *LSAT Performance with Regional, Gender, and Racial/Ethnic Breakdowns: 2001–2002 Through 2007–2008 Testing Years*, Newtown, Pa.: Law School Admission Council, LSAT Technical Report 08-03, October 2008.

DODI 1145.01—*See* U.S. Department of Defense, 2005b.

DSST, "Resources," undated. As of October 8, 2010
http://www.getcollegecredit.com/resources.html

Easi.Consult, Kenneth L. Schwartz, and Johnny J. Weismuller, *Air Force Officer Qualifying Test (AFOQT) Composite Structure Validation: Subgroup Qualification Rates—Final Report*, Randolph Air Force Base, Texas: Force Management Liaison Office, Headquarters Air Force Personnel Center, Deliverable 2, FA3089-07-0483 (FMLO-FR-2009-0001), 2008.

Edwards, N. T., "The Historical and Social Foundations of Standardized Testing: In Search of a Balance Between Learning and Evaluation," *Shiken: JALT Testing and Evaluation SIG Newsletter*, Vol. 10, No. 1, March 2006, pp. 8–16. As of August 19, 2011:
http://jalt.org/test/edw_1.htm

Eitelberg, Mark J., Janice H. Laurence, and Dianne C. Brown, "Becoming Brass: Issues in the Testing, Recruiting, and Selection of American Military Officers," in Bernard R. Gifford and Linda C. Wing, eds., *Test Policy in Defense: Lessons from the Military for Education, Training, and Employment*, Boston, Mass.: Kluwer Academic Publishers, 1992, pp. 1–141.

Excelsior College, "About Excelsior," undated (a). As of October 8, 2010:
https://www.excelsior.edu/Excelsior_College/About

———, "Credit by Exam," undated (b). As of October 8, 2010:
https://www.excelsior.edu/Excelsior_College/Excelsior_College_Examinations

Fagan, Joseph F., and Cynthia R. Holland, "Equal Opportunity and Racial Differences in IQ," *Intelligence*, Vol. 30, No. 4, July–August 2002, pp. 361–387.

———, "Racial Equality in Intelligence: Predictions from a Theory of Intelligence as Processing," *Intelligence*, Vol. 35, No. 4, 2007, pp. 319–334.

"The Few, the Proud, the Marines: The Path to Becoming a Marine Corps Officer," *MarineOfficerPrograms. com*, undated. As of September 23, 2011:
http://www.marineofficerprograms.com/pages/officer-candidate-course-occ.php

Fleming, Jacqueline, and Nancy Garcia, "Are Standardized Tests Fair to African Americans? Predictive Validity of the SAT in Black and White Institutions," *Journal of Higher Education*, Vol. 69, No. 5, September–October 1998, pp. 471–495.

Fort Bragg, "Fort Bragg OCS Application Checklist," undated.

Georgia Military College, *GMC Army ROTC Early Commissioning Program Guide*, Milledgeville, Ga., undated. As of January 7, 2010:
http://www.gmc.cc.ga.us/pdfs/ECP%20ROTC%20Guide.pdf

Gosling, Samuel D., Peter J. Rentfrow, and William B. Swann Jr., "A Very Brief Measure of the Big-Five Personality Domains," *Journal of Research in Personality*, Vol. 37, No. 6, 2003, pp. 504–528.

Green, Bert F., "A Primer of Testing," *American Psychologist*, Vol. 36, No. 10, October 1981, pp. 1001–1011.

Grogan, Jennifer, "Coast Guard Academy Graduation Is Mission: Accomplished," *Day*, May 19, 2010. As of August 17, 2010:
http://www.theday.com/article/20100519/NWS09/305199909/-1/NWS

Halsey, Ashley III, "Number of U.S. Naval Academy Graduates Becoming Marine Corps Officers Is at 10-Year High as Need Grows for Commanders in Iraq and Afghanistan," *Washington Post*, March 2, 2009. As of August 19, 2011:
http://www.washingtonpost.com/wp-dyn/content/article/2009/03/01/AR2009030102053.html

Hamm, J. James III, *Different Success Rates and Associated Factors at Three Levels of Career Progression Among U.S. Marine Corps Officers*, Monterey, Calif.: Naval Postgraduate School, master's thesis, September 1993.

Haney, Walt, "Validity, Vaudeville, and Values: A Short History of Social Concerns Over Standardized Testing," *American Psychologist*, Vol. 36, No. 10, October 1981, pp. 1021–1034.

Hardison, Chaitra M., Carra S. Sims, and Eunice C. Wong, *The Air Force Officer Qualifying Test: Validity, Fairness, and Bias*, Santa Monica, Calif.: RAND Corporation, TR-744-AF, 2010. As of August 19, 2011:
http://www.rand.org/pubs/technical_reports/TR744.html

Harrell, Thomas W., "Some History of the Army General Classification Test," *Journal of Applied Psychology*, Vol. 77, No. 6, December 1992, pp. 875–878.

Harrington, Thomas F., *Assessment of Abilities*, Greensboro, N.C.: ERIC Clearinghouse on Counseling and Student Services, ED 389960, 1995.

Hartke, Darrell D., and Lawrence O. Short, *Validity of the Academic Aptitude Composite of the Air Force Officer Qualifying Test (AFOQT)*, Brooks Air Force Base, Texas: Air Force Human Resources Laboratory, Air Force Systems Command, technical paper 87-61, April 1988.

Headquarters, Department of the Army, *Alternate Flight Aptitude Selection Test (AFAST) Information Pamphlet*, Pamphlet 611-256-2, March 1, 1987. As of December 1, 2009:
https://www.mi.ngb.army.mil/ocs/pdf/aviation/afast-study-guide.pdf

———, *United States Army Officer Candidate School*, Washington, D.C., Army Regulation 350-51, June 11, 2001. As of August 19, 2011:
http://www.apd.army.mil/pdffiles/r350_51.pdf

———, *Personnel and Classification Testing*, Washington, D.C., Army Regulation 611-5, February 5, 2008. As of August 19, 2011:
http://www.apd.army.mil/pdffiles/r611_5.pdf

Headquarters, U.S. Marine Corps, *Military Personnel Procurement Manual*, Vol. 3: *Officer Procurement*, Washington, D.C., Marine Corps Order P1100.73B, September 29, 1989. As of August 19, 2011:
http://www.marines.mil/news/publications/Documents/MCO%20P1100.73B.pdf

———, *Marine Corps Physical Fitness Test and Body Composition Program Manual*, Marine Corps Order 6100.12, May 10, 2002.

Helm, Wade R., and Jonathan D. Reid, "Race and Gender as Factors in Flight Training Success," in *Proceedings of the 45th Annual Conference of the International Military Testing Association*, Pensacola, Fla., November 3–6, 2003, pp. 123–128. As of August 19, 2011:
http://www.internationalmta.org/2003/2003Proceedings/03IMTAproceedings.pdf

Henning, Charles A., *Army Officer Shortages: Background and Issues for Congress*, Washington, D.C.: Congressional Research Service, Library of Congress, RL33518, July 5, 2006.

Hoffman, Joel M., *Significant Factors in Predicting Promotion to Major, Lieutenant Colonel, and Colonel in the United States Marine Corps*, Monterey, Calif.: Naval Postgraduate School, master's thesis, March 2008. As of August 19, 2011:
http://handle.dtic.mil/100.2/ADA479928

Hogan, Joyce C., *Physical Abilities*, Palo Alto, Calif.: Consulting Psychologists Press, 1991.

Hollenbach, Michael P., *Predictors of Plebe Summer Attrition at the United States Naval Academy*, Monterey, Calif.: Naval Postgraduate School, master's thesis, June 2003.

Hough, Leaetta M., Frederick L. Oswald, and Robert E. Ployhart, "Determinants, Detection and Amelioration of Adverse Impact in Personnel Selection Procedures: Issues, Evidence and Lessons Learned," *International Journal of Selection and Assessment*, Vol. 9, No. 1–2, March–June 2001, pp. 152–194.

Huffcutt, Allen I., James M. Conway, Philip L. Roth, and Nancy J. Stone, "Identification and Meta-Analytic Assessment of Psychological Constructs Measured in Employment Interviews," *Journal of Applied Psychology*, Vol. 86, No. 5, October 2001, pp. 897–913.

Huffcutt, Allen I., Philip L. Roth, and Michael A. McDaniel, "A Meta-Analytic Investigation of Cognitive Ability in Employment Interview Evaluations: Moderating Characteristics and Implications for Incremental Validity," *Journal of Applied Psychology*, Vol. 81, No. 5, October 1996, pp. 459–473.

Hunter, David R., and Eugene F. Burke, "Predicting Aircraft Pilot-Training Success: A Meta-Analysis of Published Research," *International Journal of Aviation Psychology*, Vol. 4, No. 4, 1994, pp. 297–313.

Hunter, John E., and Ronda F. Hunter, "Validity and Utility of Alternative Predictors of Job Performance," *Psychological Bulletin*, Vol. 96, No. 1, July 1984, pp. 72–98.

Ingerick, Michael J., *Identifying Leader Talent: Alternative Predictors for U.S. Air Force Junior Officer Selection and Assessment*, Alexandria, Va.: Human Resources Research Organization, FR-05-47, 2005.

Katz, Lawrence C., *Finding the "Right Stuff": Development of an Army Aviator Selection Instrument*, Fort Rucker, Ala.: U.S. Army Research Institute for the Behavioral and Social Sciences, November 1, 2006. As of August 19, 2011:
http://handle.dtic.mil/100.2/ADA481060

Kevles, Daniel J., "Testing the Army's Intelligence: Psychologists and the Military in World War I," *Journal of American History*, Vol. 55, No. 3, December 1968, pp. 565–581.

Kilburn, M. Rebecca, Lawrence M. Hanser, and Jacob Alex Klerman, *Estimating AFQT Scores for National Educational Longitudinal Study (NELS) Respondents*, Santa Monica, Calif.: RAND Corporation, MR-818-OSD/A, 1998. As of August 19, 2011:
http://www.rand.org/pubs/monograph_reports/MR818.html

Kleinman, Samuel D., *An Evaluation of Navy Unrestricted Line Officer Accession Programs*, Arlington, Va.: Center for Naval Analyses, Professional Paper 178, April 1977.

Knapik, Joseph J., William Rieger, Frank Palkoska, Steven Van Camp, and Salima Darakjy, "United States Army Physical Readiness Training: Rationale and Evaluation of the Physical Training Doctrine," *Journal of Strength and Conditioning Research*, Vol. 23, No. 4, July 2009, pp. 1353–1362.

Knapik, Joseph J., Marilyn A. Sharp, Bruce H. Jones, Salima Darakjy, Sarah Jones, Keith G. Hauret, and Gene Piskator, *Secular Trends in the Physical Fitness of American Youth, Young Adults, and Army Recruits*, Aberdeen Proving Ground, Md.: U.S. Army Center for Health Promotion and Preventive Medicine, August 2004. As of August 19, 2011:
http://handle.dtic.mil/100.2/ADA426849

Kobrin, Jennifer L., Brian F. Patterson, Emily J. Shaw, Krista D. Mattern, and Sandra M. Barbuti, *Validity of the SAT® for Predicting First-Year College Grade Point Average*, New York: College Board, Research Report 2008-5, October 17, 2008. As of August 19, 2011:
http://professionals.collegeboard.com/data-reports-research/cb/validity-of-sat-predicting-fycgpa

Kobrin, Jennifer L., Viji Sathy, and Emily Shaw, *A Historical View of Subgroup Performance Differences on the SAT Reasoning Test*, New York: College Board, Research Report 2006-5, January 5, 2007. As of August 19, 2011:
http://professionals.collegeboard.com/data-reports-research/cb/historical-view-sat

Koch, Charles J., *The Effect of Aviation Selection Test Battery Waivers on Marine Student-Aviator Attrition*, Monterey, Calif.: Naval Postgraduate School, master's thesis, 2009.

Korkmaz, Ibrahim, *Analysis of the Survival Patterns of United States Naval Officers*, Monterey, Calif.: Naval Postgraduate School, master's thesis, March 2005.

Kubisiak, Chris, and Lawrence C. Katz, *U.S. Army Aviator Job Analysis*, Arlington, Va.: U.S. Army Research Institute for the Behavioral and Social Sciences, Technical Report 1189, August 2006.

Kyröläinen, Heikki, Keijo Häkkinen, Hannu Kautiainen, Matti Santtila, Kai Pihlainen, and Arja Häkkinen, "Physical Fitness, BMI and Sickness Absence in Male Military Personnel," *Occupational Medicine*, Vol. 58, No. 4, 2008, pp. 251-256.

Law School Admissions Council, "About the LSAT," undated. As of August 19, 2011: http://www.lsac.org/JD/LSAT/about-the-LSAT.asp

Lee, Annette C., *The Attrition Rate at DLI*, Monterey, Calif.: Naval Postgraduate School, master's thesis, 1990.

Lehner, William D., *An Analysis of Naval Officer Accession Programs*, Monterey, Calif.: Naval Postgraduate School, master's thesis, March 2008. As of August 19, 2011: http://handle.dtic.mil/100.2/ADA479949

Leskovich, John R., *The Impact of Athletic Achievement at the United States Naval Academy on Fleet Performance*, Monterey, Calif.: Naval Postgraduate School, master's thesis, 2000. As of August 19, 2011: http://handle.dtic.mil/100.2/ADA379734

Leth, Allen D. Jr., *The Relationship Between Post Traumatic Stress and Physical Fitness and the Impact of Army Fitness Policy on Post Traumatic Stress Prevention*, Monterey, Calif.: Naval Postgraduate School, master's thesis, 2009. As of August 19, 2011: http://cgsc.contentdm.oclc.org/u?/p4013coll2,2525

Lett, John A., and F. E. O'Mara, "Predictors of Success in an Intensive Foreign Language Learning Context: Correlates of Language Learning at the Defense Language Institute Foreign Language Center," in Thomas S. Parry and Charles W. Stansfield, eds., *Language Aptitude Reconsidered*, Englewood Cliffs, N.J.: Prentice Hall Regents, 1990, pp. 222–260.

Lewinski, Robert J., and Edward J. Galway, "Psychological Services at a Naval Retraining Command," *Psychological Bulletin*, Vol. 5, No. 4, May 1945, pp. 297–300.

Lim, Nelson, Jefferson P. Marquis, Kimberly Curry Hall, David Schulker, and Xiaohui Zhuo, *Officer Classification and the Future of Diversity Among Senior Military Leaders: A Case Study of the Army ROTC*, Santa Monica, Calif.: RAND Corporation, TR-731-OSD, 2009. As of August 19, 2011: http://www.rand.org/pubs/technical_reports/TR731.html

Linn, Robert L., and C. Nicholas Hastings, "A Meta Analysis of the Validity of Predictors of Performance in Law School," *Journal of Educational Measurement*, Vol. 21, No. 3, Autumn 1984, pp. 245–259.

Lo, Ping-Hsiung, *Study of U.S. Military Officers Commissioned Through ROTC and the Service Academies*, Monterey, Calif.: Naval Postgraduate School, master's thesis, March 1997. As of August 19, 2011: http://handle.dtic.mil/100.2/ADA331664

Lohman, David F., "An Aptitude Perspective on Talent: Implications for Identification of Academically Gifted Minority Students," *Journal for the Education of the Gifted*, Vol. 28, No. 3–4, Spring 2005, pp. 333–360.

Mael, Fred A., "Staying Afloat: Within-Group Swimming Proficiency for Whites and Blacks," *Journal of Applied Psychology*, Vol. 80, No. 4, August 1995, pp. 479–490.

MARADMIN 383/10—See U.S. Marine Corps, 2010.

Mathews, John J., *Racial Equity in Selection in Air Force Officer Training School and Undergraduate Flying Training: Final Report for Period November 1974–February 1977*, Brooks Air Force Base, Texas: U.S. Department of Defense, Department of the Air Force, Air Force Systems Command, Air Force Human Resources Laboratory, Technical Report 77-22, 1977.

Mattern, Krista, Brian Patterson, Emily Shaw, Jennifer L. Kobrin, and Sandra Barbuti, *Differential Validity and Prediction of the SAT*, New York: College Board, Research Report 2008-4, October 17, 2008. As of August 19, 2011: http://professionals.collegeboard.com/data-reports-research/cb/differential-validity-prediction-sat

Mayberry, Paul W., and Catherine M. Hiatt, *Computing AFQT Scores from Historical Data*, Alexandria, Va.: Center for Naval Analyses, CRM 92-80, August 1992. As of August 19, 2011: http://handle.dtic.mil/100.2/ADA263893

McNeill, Donald B. Jr., *An Analysis of Factors Predicting Graduation at United States Marine Officer Candidates School*, Monterey, Calif.: Naval Postgraduate School, master's thesis, September 2002. As of August 19, 2011:
http://handle.dtic.mil/100.2/ADA407086

MCO 1040.43A—*See* Commandant of the Marine Corps, 2000.

MCO 1532.1—*See* Chief of Naval Operations and Commandant of the Marine Corps, 2008.

MCO 6100-12—*See* Headquarters, U.S. Marine Corps, 2002.

"Military Occupations and Implications for Racial/Ethnic and Gender Diversity: Officers," Arlington, Va., Issue Paper 23, March 2010. As of August 19, 2011:
http://mldc.whs.mil/download/documents/Issue%20Papers/23_Officer_Occupational_Choice.pdf

Moore, George L., *Low Quality Recruits: Don't Want to Go to War with Them, Can't Go Without Them—Their Impact on the All-Volunteer Force*, Fort Leavenworth, Kan.: School of Advanced Military Studies, U.S. Army Command and General Staff College, March 12, 2009. As of August 19, 2011:
http://www.dtic.mil/cgi-bin/GetTRDoc?AD=ADA513547&Location=U2&doc=GetTRDoc.pdf

Myer, Gregory J., Stephen E. Finn, Lorraine D. Eyde, Gary G. Kay, Kevin L. Moreland, Robert R. Dies, Elena J. Eisman, Tom W. Kubiszyn, and Geoffrey M. Reed, "Psychological Testing and Psychological Assessment: A Review of Evidence and Issues," *American Psychologist*, Vol. 56, No. 2, February 2001, pp. 128–165.

Naval Education and Training Command, "Officer Candidate School," referenced May 3, 2010, last modified June 23, 2011. As of February 17, 2012:
http://www.ocs.navy.mil/ocs.asp

Naval Reserve Officers Training Corps, "Scholarship Selection Criteria," last modified April 7, 2011a, referenced August 17, 2010. As of August 19, 2011:
https://www.nrotc.navy.mil/scholarship_criteria.aspx

———, "History," last modified June 27, 2011b. As of August 19, 2011:
https://www.nrotc.navy.mil/history.aspx

Naval Service Training Command, *Regulations for Officer Development (ROD) for the Naval Reserve Officers Training Corps (NROTC)*, Great Lakes, Ill., Commander of the Naval Service Training Command Instruction 1533.2, July 2, 2007. As of August 19, 2011:
https://www.netc.navy.mil/_documents/NSTCInstructions/doc77129.pdf

Noble, Julie, *The Effects of Using ACT Composite Score and High School Average on College Admission Decisions for Racial/Ethnic Groups*, Iowa City, Ia.: ACT, Research Report 2003-1, 2003.

Noble, Julie, and Richard Sawyer, *Predicting Different Levels of Academic Success in College Using High School GPA and ACT Composite Score*, Iowa City, Ia.: ACT, Research Report 2002-4, August 2002.

Nolte, Rochelle, Shawn C. Franckowiak, Carlos J. Crespo, and Ross E. Andersen, "U.S. Military Weight Standards: What Percentage of U.S. Young Adults Meet the Current Standards?" *American Journal of Medicine*, Vol. 113, No. 6, October 15, 2002, pp. 486–490.

North, James H., and Karen D. Smith, *Officer Accession Characteristics and Success at Officer Candidate School, Commissioning, and the Basic School*, Alexandria, Va.: Center for Naval Analyses, CRM 93-81.10, December 1993.

NROTC—*See* Naval Reserve Officers Training Corps.

Office of the Under Secretary of Defense, Personnel and Readiness, "FY 2006 NPS Active Component Enlisted Accessions by AFQT Category, Service, and Race/Ethnicity," Table B.5, *Population Representation in the Military Services, Fiscal Year 2006*, c. 2007.

———, *Population Representation in the Military Services: Fiscal Year 2008*, Washington, D.C., c. 2009.

———, *Population Representation in the Military Services: Fiscal Year 2009*, c. 2010.

"Officer Commissioning Programs for College Freshman [sic] Through Juniors," *MarineOfficerPrograms.com*, undated. As of September 23, 2011:
http://www.marineofficerprograms.com/pages/platoon-leaders-class-plc.php

OPNAV Instruction 1420.1B—*See* Chief of Naval Operations, 2009.

OPNAV Instruction 1532.1—*See* Chief of Naval Operations and Commandant of the Marine Corps, 2008.

Orvis, Bruce R., Michael Childress, and J. Michael Polich, *Effect of Personnel Quality on the Performance of Patriot Air Defense System Operators*, Santa Monica, Calif.: RAND Corporation, R-3901-A, 1992. As of August 19, 2011:
http://www.rand.org/pubs/reports/R3901.html

Ostoin, Steven D., *An Assessment of the Performance-Based Measurement Battery (PBMB), The Navy's Psychomotor Supplement to the Aviation Selection Test Battery (ASTB)*, Monterey, Calif.: Naval Postgraduate School, master's thesis, December 2007. As of August 19, 2011:
http://handle.dtic.mil/100.2/ADA475866

Paullin, Cheryl, Lawrence Katz, Kenneth T. Bruskiewicz, Janis Houston, and Diane Damos, *Review of Aviator Selection*, Arlington, Va.: U.S. Army Research Institute for the Behavioral and Social Sciences, Technical Report 1183, July 2006. As of August 19, 2011:
http://purl.access.gpo.gov/GPO/LPS94170

PCSM—*See* Pilot Candidate Selection Method.

Pearce, Richard R., "Effects of Cultural and Social Structural Factors on the Achievement of White and Chinese American Students at School Transition Points," *American Educational Research Journal*, Vol. 43, No. 1, Spring 2006, pp. 75–101.

Phillips, Barton L., *An Analysis of the Effect of Quantitative and Qualitative Admissions Factors in Determining Student Performance at the U.S. Naval Academy*, Monterey, Calif.: Naval Postgraduate School, master's thesis, 2004.

Pilot Candidate Selection Method, Air Education and Training Command, U.S. Air Force, home page, undated (a). As of August 19, 2011:
https://pcsm.aetc.af.mil/

———, "The PCSM Program Explained," undated (b).

———, "TBAS Information," undated (c). As of September 30, 2010:
https://pcsm.aetc.af.mil/TBASInfo.html

Ployhart, Robert E., "Staffing in the 21st Century: New Challenges and Strategic Opportunities," *Journal of Management*, Vol. 32, No. 6, December 2006, pp. 868–897.

Ployhart, Robert E., and Brian C. Holtz, "The Diversity-Validity Dilemma: Strategies for Reducing Racioethnic and Sex Subgroup Differences and Adverse Impact in Selection," *Personnel Psychology*, Vol. 61, No. 1, Spring 2008, pp. 153–172.

Polk, Christopher J., *Effective Predictors of Submarine Junior Officer Technical Competence*, Monterey, Calif.: Naval Postgraduate School, master's thesis, June 2003. As of August 19, 2011:
http://handle.dtic.mil/100.2/ADA417061

Pommerich, Mary, Daniel O. Segall, and Kathleen E. Moreno, *The Nine Lives of CAT-ASVAB: Innovations and Revelations*, presented at the U.S. Government Supported CAT Programs and Projects paper session, June 2, 2009. As of August 19, 2011:
http://www.psych.umn.edu/psylabs/catcentral/pdf%20files/cat09pommerich.pdf

Prichard, David A., and Arthur Rosenblatt, "Racial Bias in the MMPI: A Methodological Review," *Journal of Consulting and Clinical Psychology*, Vol. 48, No. 2, April 1980, pp. 263–267.

Pringle, Gloria, "Memorandum of Instruction for Division Commander's Hip Pocket Scholarships (Dedicated 2, 3, 4-Year Green to Gold Scholarships) for SY 11/12," c. 2011. As of September 23, 2011:
http://www.goarmy.com/content/dam/goarmy/downloaded_assets/pdfs/hip_pocket_moi.pdf

Public Law 80-759, Selective Service Act of 1948, June 24, 1948.

Public Law 102-166, Civil Rights Act of 1991, November 21, 1991.

Pulakos, Elaine D., and Neal Schmitt, "An Evaluation of Two Strategies for Reducing Adverse Impact and Their Effects on Criterion-Related Validity," *Human Performance*, Vol. 9, No. 9, 1996, pp. 241–258.

Putka, Dan J., ed., *Initial Development and Validation of Assessments for Predicting Disenrollment of Four-Year Scholarship Recipients from the Reserve Officer Training Corps*, Alexandria, Va.: U.S. Army Research Institute for the Behavioral and Social Sciences, Study Report 2009-06, January 2009. As of August 19, 2011: http://handle.dtic.mil/100.2/ADA495510

Pyburn, Keith M. Jr., Robert E. Ployhart, and David A. Kravitz, "The Diversity-Validity Dilemma: Overview and Legal Context," *Personnel Psychology*, Vol. 61, No. 1, Spring 2008, pp. 143–151.

Raven, John, "The Raven Progressive Matrices: A Review of National Norming Studies and Ethnic and Socioeconomic Variation Within the United States," *Journal of Educational Measurement*, Vol. 26, No. 1, Spring 1989, pp. 1–16.

Read, Robert R., and Lyn R. Whitaker, *A Data Analysis of Success in OCS, the Use of ASVAB Waivers, and Race*, Monterey, Calif.: Naval Postgraduate School, NPSOR-93-013, September 1993.

Readon, Matthew G., *The Development of Career Naval Officers from the U.S. Naval Academy: A Statistical Analysis of the Effects of Selectivity and Human Capital*, Monterey, Calif.: Naval Postgraduate School, master's thesis, 1997.

Ree, Malcolm James, and James A. Earles, "Predicting Training Success: Not Much More Than g," *Personnel Psychology*, Vol. 44, No. 2, June 1991, pp. 321–332.

Robbins, Anthony S., Susan Y. Chao, Vincent P. Fonseca, Michael R. Snedecor, and Joseph J. Knapik, "Predictors of Low Physical Fitness in a Cohort of Active-Duty U.S. Air Force Members," *American Journal of Preventive Medicine*, Vol. 20, No. 2, February 2001, pp. 90–96.

Roberts, Heather E., and Jacobina Skinner, "Gender and Racial Equity of the Air Force Officer Qualifying Test in Officer Training School Selection Decisions," *Military Psychology*, Vol. 8, No. 2, 1996, pp. 95–113.

Rodgers, William M., and William E. Spriggs, "What Does the AFQT Really Measure: Race, Wages, Schooling and the AFQT Score," *Review of Black Political Economy*, Vol. 24, No. 4, June 1996, pp. 13–46.

Rodriguez, Jacob, "Predicting the Military Career Success of United States Air Force Academy Cadets," *Armed Forces and Society*, Vol. 36, No. 1, October 2009, pp. 66–88.

Rogers, Deborah L., Bennie W. Roach, and Lawrence O. Short, *Mental Ability Testing in the Selection of Air Force Officers: A Brief Historical Overview*, Brooks Air Force Base, Texas: Air Force Human Resources Laboratory, Air Force Systems Command, Technical Paper 86-23, October 1986.

Ryabov, Igor, and Jennifer Van Hook, "School Segregation and Academic Achievement Among Hispanic Children," *Social Science Research*, Vol. 36, No. 2, June 2007, pp. 767–788.

Ryan, Ann Marie, and Nancy T. Tippins, "Attracting and Selecting: What Psychological Research Tells Us," *Human Resource Management*, Vol. 43, No. 4, Winter 2004, pp. 305–318.

Sackett, Paul R., Matthew J. Borneman, and Brian S. Connelly, "High-Stakes Testing in Higher Education and Employment: Appraising the Evidence for Validity and Fairness," *American Psychologist*, Vol. 63, No. 4, May–June 2008, pp. 215–227.

Sackett, Paul R., and Filip Lievens, "Personnel Selection," *Annual Review of Psychology*, Vol. 59, No. 1, January 2008, pp. 419–450.

Sackett, Paul R., Neal Schmitt, Jill E. Ellingson, and Melissa B. Kabin, "High-Stakes Testing in Employment, Credentialing, and Higher Education: Prospects in a Post-Affirmative-Action World," *American Psychologist*, Vol. 56, No. 4, April 2001, pp. 302–318.

Sager, Christopher E., Dan J. Putka, and Deirdre J. Knapp, "Measuring and Predicting Current and Future NCO Performance," paper presented at the 44th Annual Meeting of the International Military Testing Association, Ottawa, Canada, October 22, 2002, pp. 452–460. As of August 19, 2011: http://www.internationalmta.org/Documents/2002/Proceedings2002.pdf

Saterfiel, Thomas H., and Joyce R. McLarty, *Assessing Employability Skills*, Greensboro, N.C.: ERIC Clearinghouse on Counseling and Student Services, EDO-CG-95-21, January 30, 1995.

Schmidt, Frank L., and John E. Hunter, "The Validity and Utility of Selection Methods in Personnel Psychology: Practical and Theoretical Implications of 85 Years of Research Findings," *Psychological Bulletin*, Vol. 124, No. 2, September 1998, pp. 262–274.

Schmitt, Alicia P., "Language and Cultural Characteristics That Explain Differential Item Functioning for Hispanic Examinees on the Scholastic Aptitude Test," *Journal of Educational Measurement*, Vol. 25, No. 1, March 1988, pp. 1–13.

Schmitt, Alicia P., and Neil J. Dorans, "Differential Item Functioning for Minority Examinees on the SAT," *Journal of Educational Measurement*, Vol. 27, No. 1, Spring 1990, pp. 67–81.

Schmitt, Neal, and David Chan, *Personnel Selection: A Theoretical Approach*, Thousand Oaks, Calif.: Sage Publications, 1998.

Schrader, W. B., "Summary of Law School Validity Studies, 1948–1975 (Report No. LSAC-76-8)," in Law School Admission Council, *Reports of the LSAC Sponsored Research*, Vol. III: *1975–1977*, Princeton, N.J., 1977, pp. 519–550.

Schwind, David A., *A Qualitative Analysis of Selection to Flag Rank in the United States Navy*, Monterey, Calif.: Naval Postgraduate School, master's thesis, June 2004. As of August 19, 2011:
http://handle.dtic.mil/100.2/ADA424782

Sheppard, Thomas A., *A Validation of the Strong Campbell Interest Inventory as Part of the Admissions Process at the United States Naval Academy*, Monterey, Calif.: Naval Postgraduate School, master's thesis, 2002.

Smith, Elizabeth P., and Scott E. Graham, *Validation of Psychomotor and Perceptual Predictors of Armor Officer M-1 Gunnery Performance*, Alexandria, Va.: U.S. Army Research Institute for the Behavioral and Social Sciences, Technical Report 766, November 1987. As of August 19, 2011:
http://handle.dtic.mil/100.2/ADA191333

Smith, Monte D., and Joseph D. Hagman, *Enhancing Officer Candidate School (OCS) Enrollment in the Army National Guard (ARNG)*, Alexandria, Va.: U.S. Army Research Institute for the Behavioral and Social Sciences, Research Report 1797, October 2002.

Society for Industrial and Organizational Psychology and American Psychological Association Division of Industrial-Organizational Psychology, *Principles for the Validation and Use of Personnel Selection Procedures*, Bowling Green, Ohio, 2003.

Strein, William, *Assessment of Self-Concept*, Greensboro, N.C.: ERIC Clearinghouse on Counseling and Student Services, EDO-CG-95-14, 1995.

Talbot, Laura A., Ali A. Weinstein, and Jerome L. Fleg, "Army Physical Fitness Test Scores Predict Coronary Heart Disease Risk in Army National Guard Soldiers," *Military Medicine*, Vol. 174, No. 3, March 2009, pp. 245–252.

Tan, Michelle, "Air Force Cancels Another Non-Rated OTS Board," *Air Force Times*, April 24, 2010. As of July 6, 2010:
http://www.airforcetimes.com/news/2010/04/airforce_ots_board_042410w/

Taylor, Marcus K., Amanda E. Markham, Jared P. Reis, Genieleah A. Padilla, Eric G. Potterat, Sean P. A. Drummond, and Lilianne R. Mujica-Parodi, "Physical Fitness Influences Stress Reactions to Extreme Military Training," *Military Medicine*, Vol. 173, No. 8, 2008, pp. 738–742. As of August 19, 2011:
http://www.dtic.mil/cgi-bin/GetTRDoc?Location=U2&doc=GetTRDoc.pdf&AD=ADA497022

U.S. Air Force, "General Norton A. Schwartz," August 2009. As of January 10, 2011:
http://www.af.mil/information/bios/bio.asp?bioID=7077

———, "Jeanne M. Holm Center for Officer Accessions and Citizen Development," November 23, 2010; referenced July 7, 2010. As of August 19, 2011:
http://www.af.mil/information/factsheets/factsheet.asp?id=13032

U.S. Air Force Academy, "Preparing for the Academy," undated (a).

———, "Welcome to the U.S. Air Force Academy Visitor Center!" undated (b). As of August 20, 2010:
http://www.usafa.edu/superintendent/pa/visitor-center.cfm?catname=Visiting%20USAFA

———, Plans, Programs and Institutional Events, "Demographic Profile of the Class of 2013," July 9, 2009. As of July 9, 2009:
https://admissions.usafa.edu/RRC/Class_of_2013_profile.pdf

U.S. Air Force Reserve Officer Training Corps, "Apply/Track Applications," undated (a). As of September 23, 2011:
http://www.afrotc.com/scholarships/application/

———, "High School Scholarships," undated (b). As of August 17, 2010:
http://afrotc.com/scholarships/high-school/eligibility/

———, "High School Scholarships," undated (c). As of August 17, 2010:
http://www.afrotc.com/scholarships/high-school/process-description/

———, "Mission and Values," undated (d). As of November 9, 2009:
http://www.afrotc.com/learn-about/mission-and-values/

———, "Requirements and Standards," undated (e). As of August 17, 2010:
http://afrotc.com/admissions/requirements-standards/fitness/

U.S. Army, "Army ROTC: Enlisted Soldiers," undated (a). As of May 10, 2010:
http://www.goarmy.com/rotc/enlisted-soldiers.html

———, "Army ROTC: Legacy and Value," undated (b). As of August 19, 2011:
http://www.goarmy.com/rotc/legacy-and-value.html

———, "Officer Candidate School," undated (c). As of August 19, 2011:
http://www.goarmy.com/ocs.html

U.S. Army Garrison Benelux, "CLEP DSST Excelsior: Testing for College Credit," October 23, 2007. As of October 5, 2010:
http://www.garrisonchievres.eur.army.mil/sites/services/docs/Trifold_Nov07.pdf

U.S. Army Recruiting Command, "Army Physical Fitness Testing," undated.

U.S. Army Reserve Officer's Training Corps, home page, undated (a). As of November 9, 2009:
http://www.goarmy.com/rotc.html

———, Southern Illinois University Carbondale, Saluki Strike Battalion, "Becoming an Officer," undated (b). As of July 18, 2010:
http://www.armyrotc.com/edu/southernilcarbondale/becominganofficer.htm

USCGA—See U.S. Coast Guard Academy.

U.S. Coast Guard, "Coast Guard 2010 Snapshot," undated (a).

———, "Officer Candidate School," undated (b). As of July 18, 2010:
http://www.gocoastguard.com/find-your-career/officer-opportunities/programs/officer-candidate-school

———, "Careers," last modified October 27, 2010; referenced August 17, 2010. As of August 19, 2011:
http://www.uscg.mil/top/careers.asp

———, "College Level Examination Program (CLEP)," last modified July 22, 2011. As of October 5, 2010:
http://www.uscg.mil/hq/capemay/Education/clep.asp

U.S. Coast Guard Academy, home page, undated (a). As of July 5, 2010:
http://www.uscga.edu

———, "Application Process," undated (b). As of September 23, 2011:
http://www.cga.edu/display.aspx?id=2950

———, "International Cadets: Language Assessment," undated (c). As of October 8, 2010:
http://www.uscga.edu/display.aspx?id=2916

———, "Leadership Development Center," undated (d); referenced July 18, 2010. As of August 24, 2011:
http://www.cga.edu/LDC_display.aspx?id=648

———, "Cadet Candidate Physical Fitness Examination: Instruction Manual and Scoring Table," New London, Conn., revised August 10, 2010. As of August 18, 2011:
http://www.uscga.edu/uploadedFiles/Admissions/AcademyAdmissions/AcademyAdmission_subs/2015%20PFE%20Manual.pdf

U.S. Coast Guard Training Center, *Officer Program Application Preparation Handbook (OCS, CSPI, PPEP, DCE, and AVCAD)*, Vol. 10, Cape May, N.J., June 2010. As of August 27, 2011:
http://www.uscg.mil/hq/capemay/education/doc/Booklet01.pdf

U.S. Code, Title 29, Labor, Chapter XIV, Equal Employment Opportunity Commission, Part 1607, Uniform Guidelines on Employee Selection Procedures. As of August 22, 2011:
http://www.access.gpo.gov/nara/cfr/waisidx_10/29cfr1607_10.html

U.S. Department of Defense, *Defense Language Transformation Roadmap*, January 2005a. As of August 19, 2011:
http://www.defense.gov/news/Mar2005/d20050330roadmap.pdf

———, *Qualitative Distribution of Military Manpower*, Instruction 1145.01, September 20, 2005b. As of October 4, 2010:
http://www.dtic.mil/whs/directives/corres/pdf/114501p.pdf

———, *Commissioned Officer Promotion Reports (COPRs)*, Instruction 1320.13, July 22, 2009. As of August 19, 2011:
http://www.dtic.mil/whs/directives/corres/pdf/132013p.pdf

U.S. Government Accountability Office, *Military Personnel: Strategic Plan Needed to Address Army's Emerging Officer Accession and Retention Challenges—Report to the Committee on Armed Services, House of Representatives*, Washington, D.C., GAO-07-224, January 2007. As of August 19, 2011:
http://purl.access.gpo.gov/GPO/LPS80094

U.S. Marine Corps, "Commissioning Programs," undated (a). As of July 18, 2010:
http://officer.marines.com/marine/making_marine_officers/commissioning_programs

———, "Commissioning Sources," undated (b); referenced July 8, 2011.

——— "Marine Officer Programs," undated (c).

———, "2010 ECP, MCP, MCP-R AND RECP Selection Board Results," Marine Administrative Message 383/10, July 13, 2010. As of October 4, 2010:
http://www.usmc.mil/news/messages/Pages/MARADMIN383-10.aspx

U.S. Merchant Marine Academy, "Candidate Fitness Assessment Instructions," undated. As of August 18, 2011:
http://www.usmma.edu/admissions/PDFs/CFA_Instructions05.pdf

U.S. Military Academy at West Point, home page, undated (a); referenced July 18, 2010. As of August 24, 2011:
http://www.usma.edu/

———, "Class of 2013," undated (b). As of August 19, 2011:
http://www.usma.edu/class/2013/profile.asp

U.S. Military Entrance Processing Command, *Counselor's Manual for the Armed Services Vocational Aptitude Battery Form-14, Technical Supplement*, North Chicago, Ill., DOD-1304.12X1; USMEPCOM/RPI-CODE-003, 1985.

USNA—*See* U.S. Naval Academy.

U.S. Naval Academy, home page, undated (a); referenced July 18, 2010. As of August 24, 2011:
http://www.usna.edu

———, "Class Portrait 2013," undated (b). As of August 20, 2010:
http://www.usna.edu/admissions/documents/Class%20Portrait%202013.pdf

U.S. Navy, "NROTC," undated (a), referenced November 9, 2009. As of February 17, 2012:
http://www.navy.com/joining/education-opportunities/nrotc/

———, "Qualifications and Commitment," undated (b). As of July 18, 2010:
http://www.navy.com/navy/joining/qualifications.html

———, "OCS Enhances Curriculum, Increases Class Size," March 11, 2010. As of May 3, 2010:
http://www.navy.mil/search/display.asp?story_id=51782

U.S. v. Virginia, 518 U.S. 515, 1996.

Welsh, John R., Susan K. Kucinkas, and Linda T. Curran, *Armed Services Vocational Battery (ASVAB): Integrative Review of Validity Studies*, Brooks Air Force Base, Texas: Air Force Human Resources Laboratory, Air Force Systems Command, Technical Report 90-22, 1990.

Whitmarsh, Patrick J., and Robert H. Sulzen, "Prediction of Simulated Infantry-Combat Performance from a General Measure of Individual Aptitude," *Military Psychology*, Vol. 1, No. 2, 1989, pp. 111–116.

Wiener, Solomon, *Military Flight Aptitude Tests*, 6th ed., Lawrenceville, N.J.: Thomson/Arco, 2005.

Wilson, Kenneth M., *A Review of Research on the Prediction of Academic Performance After the Freshman Year*, New York: College Entrance Examination Board, Research Report 83-11, 1983.

Winkler, John D., Judith C. Fernandez, and J. Michael Polich, *Effect of Aptitude on the Performance of Army Communications Operators*, Santa Monica, Calif.: RAND Corporation, R-4143-A, 1992. As of August 19, 2011:
http://www.rand.org/pubs/reports/R4143.html

Wise, Lauress, John Welsh, Frances Grafton, Paul Foley, James Earles, Linda Sawin, and D. R. Divgi, "Sensitivity and Fairness of the Armed Services Vocational Aptitude Battery (ASVAB) Technical Composites," Personnel Testing Division, Defense Manpower Data Center, Department of Defense, December 1992.

Wiskoff, Martin F., and Glenn M. Rampton, eds., *Military Personnel Measurement: Testing, Assignment, Evaluation*, New York: Praeger, 1989.

Young, John W., *Differential Validity, Differential Prediction, and College Admission Testing: A Comprehensive Review and Analysis*, New York: College Board, January 1, 2001. As of August 19, 2011:
http://professionals.collegeboard.com/data-reports-research/cb/differential-validity-prediction

Zeidner, Joseph, Cecil Johnson, Yefim Vladimirsky, and Susan Weldon, *Fairness of Army ASVAB Test Composites for MOS and Job Families*, Alexandria, Va.: U.S. Army Research Institute for the Behavioral and Social Sciences, 2004. As of August 19, 2011:
http://handle.dtic.mil/100.2/ADA422165